APPROACHES TO LITERATURE

Gilbert Vaughan

APPROACHES TO LITERATURE

A Practical Handbook for Beginners

WSC PRESS - *Wayne, Ne*

Approaches to Literature: A Practical Handbook for Beginners
Copyright © 2012, 2020 by Gilbert Vaughan
All Rights Reserved

ISBN 978-0-9766513-2-1

4th Printing, 2020

Published by WSC Press

Editors: Maureen Kingston, Tyisha J.E. Wrice, Elijah Herrington
Production Editor: Eddie Elfers
Managing Editor: Chad Christensen
Cover: Lessing J. Rosenwald Collection, Library of Congress.
Copyright © 2005 The William Blake Archive. Used with permission.

WSC Press
1111 Main Street
Wayne, NE 68787

wscpress@wsc.edu
wscpress.com

TABLE OF CONTENTS

PREFACE

Most people who choose to read books, rather than read them because someone else assigned them in a course, would probably say that they read because they enjoy reading. Even critics, beginning with Aristotle, have emphasized the double purpose of literature: to teach and to entertain. The most common approach to literature, even among graduate students in an advanced literature class, if free to discuss what they want, is to discuss what one likes or dislikes about a literary work. So why analyze literature? Why apply complex approaches to literature? Why not just enjoy it?

I don't think that applying different approaches to literary works destroys the pleasure of reading them. However complex the approach, whatever games we may play, a good book retains its power to engulf us in its world. At the same time, no reading is passive. Our minds are always active as we read, noticing implausibilities in a work of fiction, savoring the irony of the narrator's comments, figuring out the complexities of the plot, noticing the shifts in point of view, tracing the different meanings of symbols. Consciously applying different approaches to a piece of literature may deepen our understanding of the work. And each approach may exercise our intellect, give us different ways of thinking about life and about literature. Diverse approaches give us methods and tools to formulate ideas and analyses.

When did literary criticism begin? Our earliest critics are the Greeks, Plato and Aristotle. Aristotle wrote the first formal literary criticism, giving us terms like plot and character. But Aristotle probably did not form his critical principles from scratch. His criticism must go back to earlier critics. If we try to imagine the first critics of literature, we have to remember that literature was at first oral; the first creators of literature were people who told stories to audiences—audiences who must have asked questions and discussed the stories among themselves. We can also imagine the storytellers forming rules and patterns of stories as they discussed the storytelling process among themselves and passed down their stories and traditions of storytelling to younger storytellers. Thus, analyzing and discussing literature has probably always accompanied the enjoyment of literature. Perhaps analysis is even part of the pleasure of literature. This book attempts to summarize and explain some basic approaches to literature, some traditional and some modern. It is designed for beginning students of literature and introduces them to different ways of reading and interpreting literature. Each chapter presents an approach in clear and direct terms. Most chapters contain essays showing how one might apply the approach to a piece of literature. Most chapters have questions at the end or where appropriate for discussion and writing. Each chapter is meant to be an independent unit and can be read in any order, though most people might want to start with the first chapter which emphasizes the authors and their place in literary history and the genre chapters on fiction, poetry, and drama before moving on to the other more modern approaches.

I have selected approaches that work well with students in an introductory literature class. Nowadays, there are as many approaches as there are critics, and if one were to present all the important current literary approaches, one would have an encyclopedia, not a handbook.

Although this handbook could be used with an anthology, it is designed primarily for courses in which teachers choose their own books.

—Gilbert Vaughan

APPROACHES TO LITERATURE

1

TRADITIONAL APPROACH TO LITERATURE

THE AUTHOR'S LIFE AND CONTEXT

One of the most common approaches to literature, still popular today, is studying the lives and times of writers and examining their place in literary history. Since writers, of course, write primarily out of their own experience, readers are curious about how writers' lives and personalities have affected their work and how writers have used their experiences in their writing. Readers sometimes feel a need to see literary works as autobiographical expressions; they want to find the real person behind the work. Unfortunately, or fortunately, depending on one's point of view, we frequently know little or nothing about the writers. We know absolutely nothing about Homer, except that he was probably an oral poet. We know some of the facts about Shakespeare's life—he married a woman older than he was himself, he acted as well as wrote plays, he owned property in Stratford and left the second-best bed to his wife—but we have very little idea of Shakespeare, the individual. And we may know so much that we find ourselves spending all our time emphasizing the authors' lives and neglecting their works. One could spend a lifetime not only studying James Joyce's works but also his life. But whether we know just a little or have volumes of letters, journals, and biographies, most readers find some information about the writers' lives helpful in understanding their writing.

Knowing something about the historical period and culture in which writers lived is also helpful. The most accessible book to contemporary readers is likely to be a contemporary novel from their own culture. Reading a Victorian novel is easier if one knows something about 19th century England, although one may also learn about the history and culture of a period by reading a novel. Another approach is to analyze how writers fit into literary history. What earlier writers have authors read, and how did they influence their writing? Are authors part of a literary movement? Are the authors rebelling against a dominant movement or trend? How much are authors typical or representative writers of their time, and how original are the authors? What influence did authors have in their own time and in later times?

Since throughout this book I will use poems from William Blake's *Songs of Innocence* and *Songs of Experience*, the rest of the chapter will be devoted to Blake, focusing on his life and times from his birth to the writing of these poems.

THE LIFE AND TIMES OF WILLIAM BLAKE (1757-1827)

William Blake was born November 28, 1757, in London, where except for a couple of years he lived all of his life. London in the 18th century was the financial, political, and cultural center of England, but also a place of great poverty, disease, and crime. Blake's poem "London" as well as other poems in *Songs of Experience* gives us glimpses of the suffering of the poor any person wandering through the streets might observe, especially the misery and exploitation of children and of prostitutes. According to Blake's most recent biographer, James King, the neighborhood where Blake grew up, Picadilly, was "an uneasy mixture of opulence and destitution" (2). Here both the rich and the poor lived. There were fine shops and homes, but nearby were a slaughterhouse and a workhouse with up to 300 people as well as beggars and mad dogs and piles of manure in the streets. His father, James Blake, was a shopkeeper, a hosier and a haberdasher, who worked hard to establish a successful business. William was the third of seven children (two of whom died as infants). James Blake was a dissenter from the Church of England, a Baptist. William's parents seem to have been devoted and caring, though Blake was not the favorite and felt some resentment toward his other brothers and felt somewhat alienated from the rest of the family. King describes him as "obviously opinionated, questioning, rebellious, and sometimes obdurate and saucy" (7).

According to an early biographer, Frederick Tatham (quoted in *Blake Records*), even as a child Blake possessed a "daring impetuous & vigorous temper ... Although easily persuaded, he despised restraints & rules, so much that his Father dared not send him to School. Like the Arabian Horse, he is said to have so hated a Blow that his Father thought it most prudent to withhold from him the liability of receiving punishment. He picked up his Education where he could" (510). His mother probably taught him to read and write. It is evident that Blake read widely; he knew the Bible, Shakespeare, and Milton thoroughly. Although he spent most of his life in the city, as a boy he was close enough to the country to walk in the woods and swim naked in the ponds.

As a child he saw visions. An early biographer, Alexander Gilchrist, describes his first vision at the age of eight or nine:

Sauntering along, the boy looks up, and sees a tree filled with angels, bright angelic wings bespangling every bough like stars. Returned he relates the incident, and only through his mother's intercession escapes a thrashing from his honest father, for telling a lie. Another time one summer morn he sees the haymakers at work and amid them angelic figures walking (BR 7).

He continued to see visions all his life, though he probably considered them the result of an active and very vivid imagination. He answered a lady once who asked him where he saw a vision thus: "*Here,* madam," he answered, touching his forehead. His imagination was so strong that he seemed able to see physically what he imagined.

As a child he early showed an interest in both art and poetry. He liked drawing, which his mother secretly encouraged. His father gave him money to buy prints and bought for him plaster casts of ancient statuary. He wrote poetry by the age of twelve. At the age of ten he took lessons at Henry Pars' academy, where mainly the students copied prints and casts. At fourteen, he was apprenticed to James Basire, an engraver. For the next seven years, he studied the art of engraving, probably continuing his literary education from the books they engraved—books of history, mythology, and poetry.

When he completed his apprenticeship, Blake was able to make a good living, engraving and painting watercolors, although he did suffer from poverty in later years. He studied for a few years at the Royal Academy and made friends with other artists. He married Catherine Boucher (or Butcher) when he was 25. He seems to have married her on the rebound when another woman rejected him. She may have been illiterate at the time of marriage (she signed the register with an X); if so, Blake educated her, for she was able to help him with his work. They seemed very devoted to each other. There is a story about how they would sit naked in their garden and recite Paradise Lost. Partly because they had no children and since she worked with him in his business, they developed a deep and close relationship. The only story that shows some discord between them concerns Blake's favorite brother Robert. During an argument between Robert and Catherine, Blake interrupted them and said to Catherine, "Kneel down and beg Robert's pardon directly, or you never see my face again!" (*BR* 30). Robert took the blame himself and stopped the quarrel.

The death of his brother Robert in 1787 was the most shattering experience of his life. Blake was nine years older than Robert. He had always given Robert the love and affection and companionship that he gave to no one else in his family. He felt fatherly toward him and was tutoring him to be an artist. He stayed by Robert's bedside night and day until he died. At the moment of death he saw Robert's "released spirit ascend heavenward through the matter-of-fact ceiling, clapping its hands for joy" (*BR* 32). Robert's death led Blake to reexamine his life and art. He decided to become a poet-engraver, combining his poetry with his art. He said that Robert appeared to him in a dream, giving him the secret of a technique for combining "song and design." In a letter to a friend several years later he wrote about the influence that this brother continued to have on him: "Thirteen years ago I lost a brother & with his spirit I converse daily & hourly in the Spirit & See him in my remembrance in the regions of my Imagination. I hear his advice now & even write from his Dictate" (*Letters* 43).

From about 1789 to 1794 Blake worked on his *Songs of Innocence and Songs of Experience*. His method was unique: he combined illustration and text to create a work that was both literature and art, "song and design." For example, in the first page of "The Ecchoing Green" (quoted below), the handwritten text is surrounded by vines. At the right of the first stanza stands a boy with a hoop; on the left a boy is playing with a hoop. At the top of the page a large green umbrella-like tree shelters two mothers with two small children each and several old people. The illustrations plus the words create a vision of happy people taking pleasure in life and in each other. Blake engraved, printed, and then colored each picture-poem. Each copy of the *Songs* is different, and the colors may vary considerably. (See www.blakearchive.org for examples of Blake's illustrations.)

Any short biographical sketch can only give a glimpse into the life of a complex person. For a closer look into Blake's inner life, here is a passage from a letter to a man who objected to one of Blake's paintings:

> Fun I love, but too much Fun is of all things the most loathsom. Mirth is better than Fun, & Happiness is better than Mirth. I feel that a Man may be happy in this World. And I know that This World is a World of imagination & Vision. I see Every thing that I paint In This World, but Every body does not see alike ... But to the Eyes of the Man of Imagination, Nature is Imagination itself. As a man is. So he Sees. As the Eye is formed, such are its Powers. You certainly Mistake, when you say that the Visions of Fancy are not to be found in This World. To Me This World is all One continued Vision of Fancy or Imagination ... (*Letters* 35-36).

Although Blake was not very active politically, he was at least a revolutionary in his thinking and in his art. He supported the American Revolution, seeing it as a struggle for freedom; he sympathized with the French Revolution until its excesses turned him against it as it did other English writers. He saw both the state and the church, formal government and organized religion, as institutions that crushed and repressed human beings. In the "Preface" to *Milton,* the last stanza (which became the gospel song of the socialists in the 20th century), sums up his determination to work for creating the ideal society on earth:

> I will not cease from Mental Fight.
> Nor shall my Sword sleep in my hand
> Till we have built Jerusalem
> In England's green & pleasant land.

WILLIAM BLAKE'S PLACE IN LITERARY HISTORY

William Blake, both the artist and the poet, was little known or appreciated in his own time. It was not until 1927, the centenary of his death, that his reputation was established and he became part of the literary canon. Now his poems are included in all the anthologies of British literature and most general anthologies; a room in the Tate Gallery in London is devoted to his paintings. While Blake's later long poems, the prophetic books, like the Songs (a combination of poem and design) are studied in advanced literary classes, it is his *Songs of Innocence* and *Songs of Experience* that are most popular with readers and critics. These poems were all written in the 18th century before the Romantic movement started in England, but except for their simplicity of language and metrics (reminiscent of Elizabethan poetry) these poems seem to belong to a new age. Blake was a poet with his own unique vision; he was a loner who didn't feel himself a part of any movement. As far as we know, he did not read Wordsworth and Coleridge, the founders of the Romantic movement in England, and he did not influence them, though we know that Coleridge owned a copy of the *Songs.* Yet almost all anthologies of the English Romantic period begin with Blake, and the characteristics of the Romantic period can be found in his poems.

The Romantic poets were, first of all, reacting against the ideas of the neo-classical age, the age of Reason. Instead of putting the emphasis on reason, on order and balance, the romantics emphasized emotion, the irrational. Instead of seeking for the golden mean, which in the 18th century consisted of keeping emotions under the control of reason, Blake said in one of the proverbs from *The Marriage of Heaven and Hell*, "The road of excess leads to the palace of wisdom," and, "You never know what is enough unless you know what is more than enough." His most extreme proverb suggests the danger of repressing emotion: "Sooner murder an infant in its cradle than nurse unacted desires." The Romantics believed that one should follow one's heart and instincts—one's desires. One's desires could be trusted because they believed that people were basically good unless they had been corrupted by civilization which taught them to distrust themselves and put their faith in the church and the state, institutions that Blake felt destroyed the individual. The Romantics stressed the individual, the person, rather than the general type, Man. Literature was an exploration of the individual, his or her experience and inner life. The individual was always striving for a more complete life, for perfection, for that which cannot ultimately be obtained. The striving, the seeking, became the goal itself.

The Romantics are known for their love of Nature. Nature was a place where one could escape from the pressures of the everyday world and commune with one's soul—and with God. The Romantics sometimes had a pantheistic concept of nature—the belief that all nature is one, all a part of God. Blake is not usually considered a nature poet, but the first stanza of "The Ecchoing Green" gives us a picture of happy people participating in nature, their sports a part of the harmony and unity and joy of nature, the shouts of the players blending in with the sound of the bells and of the birds:

> The Sun does arise,
> And Make happy the skies.
> The merry bells ring,
> To welcome the Spring.
> The Sky-lark and thrush,
> The birds of the bush,
> Sing louder around,
> To the bells' cheerful sound,
> While our sports shall be seen
> On the Ecchoing Green.

The Romantics, especially Wordsworth, wanted to portray the everyday life of ordinary people. Blake's *Songs* also tell the individual stories of chimney sweepers, schoolboys, and nurses. In the second and final stanzas of "The Ecchoing Green," ordinary people play together, spontaneously enjoying life, not bothered by duty or reason. Old John, sitting among the old people, remembers the joys of his own youth as the old people laugh and vicariously participate in the children's play. Night, which brings an end to day and perhaps symbolically of life, is not threatening but comforting. The poem is a Romantic celebration of the unity of life: the old and young, nature and people, morning and sunset, life and death.

> Old John with white hair
> Does laugh away care,
> Sitting under the oak,
> Among the old folk.
> They laugh at our play,
> And soon they all say,
> Such such were the joys,
> When we all girls and boys,
> In our youth time were seen,
> On the Ecchoing Green.
> Till the little ones weary
>
> No more can be merry
> The sun does descend,
> And our sports have an end:
> Round the laps of their mothers,
> Many sisters and brothers,
> Like birds in their nest,
> Are ready for rest:
> And sport no more seen,
> On the darkening Green.

The Romantics asserted the importance of the imagination but none more than Blake. His literary and artistic works are an expression of his inner vision, his intuitive understanding of the ideal world he created in his mind.

Blake can be seen as a Romantic poet: his poems reflect the times—the period of the French Revolution, in particular. But, like all good writers, he has his own unique way of writing—he is his own kind of Romantic poet, like no other.

Works Cited

Bentley. G.E., Jr. *Blake Records*. [*BR*]. Oxford: Oxford University Press, 1969.
King, James. *William Blake: His Life*. New York: St. Martin's Press, 1991.
The Letters of William Blake. ed. Geoffrey Keynes. New York: The Macmillan Company, 1956.

2

FORMALIST APPROACH TO LITERATURE & GENRE APPROACH TO POETRY

FORMALIST CRITICS

Formalist critics, sometimes called New Critics in America, emphasize the close study of a literary text. They consider the literary text—a novel, short story, poem—as an aesthetic object, a work of art.

Formalist critics, who began forming their critical theories in the early 1920s, are reacting against the traditional methods of literary criticism. They oppose the study of literature based on the author's life. They believe that a literary work should not be read to illustrate how the author's life influenced her or his work or how the work reflects the writer's life. Instead, they analyze each work as a separate piece of art.

They also are not interested in seeing the literary work as part of a culture. They ignore, as far as possible, the historical and social background of a work. They are not interested in the part a literary work plays in the history of literature or even in the history of ideas. They are not interested in sources authors have used in writing their texts or in the influence of earlier writers or works. They try to analyze the literary object as a self-contained unit.

Since they are interested only in the literary work of art, they are not concerned with the author's intentions. They see the finished work of art as separate even from its creator. One never asks, "What did the writer intend?" or "What did the writer mean?" To ask these questions is to commit **the intentional fallacy** defined by W.K. Wimsatt and Monroe C. Beardsley as a "confusion between the poem and its origins." How the author wrote or what the author intended is irrelevant to the examination of the completed work of art. Wimsatt and Beardsley, like other New Critics, also want readers to avoid **the affective fallacy,** which is "the confusion between the poem and its results." That is, the formalist critic usually avoids the analysis of the psychological effect of the poem on the reader; the critic does not ask, for example, how a poem affects the reader or what emotions it arouses. Critical judgment, Wimsatt and Beardsley say, disappears as individual readers devote themselves to their subjective impressions of poems. These critics are not interested in readers' emotional responses to a literary work.

Another fallacy, or even worse, is what Cleanth Brooks calls "the heresy of paraphrase." To paraphrase a poem is to translate it into other words—to restate the poem in prose. One definition of poetry is "that which cannot be translated." The exact words in the exact order as the author wrote them is what makes the poem; to rephrase the poem in other words is to lose the poem. One can analyze a poem and how it works but no analysis can exhaust a poem. The formalist critics also oppose reducing the poem to some abstract statement or moral. The poem is a complex work of art; to paraphrase it or reduce it to a generalization denies its artistic integrity.

What the formalist critic tries to do is to study and evaluate the work of art as a whole, as a unity. As a tree is composed of leaves, branches, roots, and a trunk, so a poem is a whole but also consists of images, metaphors, rhythm, and symbols, all creating a unified object of art. If one is analyzing a short story, one considers how the plot, the characterization, the setting, the point of view, and the style all contribute to the unity of the story. As far as possible, one does not try to separate form from content. If one reduces the poem to its content, to its subject matter, one loses the poem and gets an abstraction or moral instead. "That in a successful work, form and content cannot be separated" is one of the basic tenets expressed by Cleanth Brooks in "The Formalist Critics." He insists that "form is meaning." What the formalist critic does is to analyze the patterns and the devices of the poem (the images, metaphors, rhyme, sound, etc.) in order to see how these aspects of the poem relate to the whole. The critic analyzes, as Brooks says, "the relation of various parts to each other in building up the whole." Brooks also stresses that poets express "the universal and general" through "the concrete and the particular" (or one might say the content is expressed through the form).

Brooks suggests that one should think of a poem as a drama in which the conflicts, tensions, opposites are resolved into a unity by the end of a successful poem. One should ask, What problems does the poem present, and how does it solve the problems?

Literature, says Brooks, is "ultimately metaphorical and symbolic." A scientist writes as clearly as possible in order to convey information; an artist communicates feelings, attitudes, interpretations—not facts. The factual writer is primarily interested in the **denotative** use of words—the literal, specific, exact dictionary meaning. Literary artists stress **connotative** use of words. Literary artists use words to suggest, evoke, stimulate, puzzle, probe, gladden, even confuse. A poet uses metaphors, similes, irony, rhyme, and other poetic devices to express human values and concerns. The scientist might clinically describe death; the poet exclaims: "or ever the silver card be loosed, /or the golden bowl be broken …" The poet of Ecclesiastes suggests by his images of silver cards and golden bowl both how precious life is and how fragile, making us see more than just the fact of death.

Poets use **irony** (stating the opposite of what they mean or giving the words a double meaning, making contradictory statements) and **ambiguity** (using words to suggest different meanings at the same time) and other devices to give a complex sense of human reality. The critic analyzes how the poet uses words to create the whole work of art.

To sum up, the formalist critic is primarily interested in examining and carefully analyzing a literary text. The critic insists on a close reading. (Formalist teachers may explode with wrath at students who do not follow the text as they talk about it.)

Finally, one must stress the limitations of the formalist approach. The formalist isolates the work of art from its cultural background and, in the process, loses part of what one needs to understand and appreciate the work of art fully. When analyzing a literary work, most modern critics will pay some attention to the historical period in which it was written. To read a work in complete isolation from its cultural context is an artificial, if not impossible, activity.

FORMALIST TERMS FOR ANALYZING POETRY

Most of the following will refer primarily to poetry, though some terms can be applied to other forms of literature. Perhaps, we need a technical definition of poetry that will separate it from prose. Poetry consists of sentences arranged by lines rather than put in paragraph form as in prose. Thus, a poem is a form of literature that consists of lines or verses rather than paragraphs. One can tell by a glance whether the writer of a work intended it to be a poem.

The Speaker And Figures Of Speech

SPEAKER or PERSONA—the "I" of the poem. One might think of the speaker as the character the author uses to speak the poem. One should never identify the speaker with the author, just as one should not identify the narrator of a story with the author. All we know about the speaker comes from the poem itself. The term **persona** suggests the mask or the actor the author uses to speak the words. The speakers may tell us something about themselves, their lives and personalities, or they may just give us a mood, an attitude, an opinion, a reaction. The formalist critic always looks at each poem of an author's individually when identifying and analyzing the speaker.

IMAGE—a concrete detail that appeals to one of our senses: to sight, smell, taste, sound, touch.

Note the imagery in the first stanza of William Blake's "The Ecchoing Green":

> The Sun does arise,
> And make happy the skies.
> And merry bells ring,
> To welcome the Spring.
> The Sky-lark and thrush,
> The birds of the bush,
> Sing louder around,
> To the bells' cheerful sound,
> While our sports shall be seen
> On the Ecchoing Green.

You can see the sun rise and the children playing sports on the green grass and probably the birds; you can hear the bells ring and the birds sing and the sounds the playing children make as their voices echo on the green. All the images suggest harmony and joy in this little world of the green—where the sun makes happy skies under which the children's voices and the "cheerful" and "merry" bells and the singing of the birds all join in to celebrate spring.

SIMILE—a comparison using *like* or *as* or *than*. (Items compared must be from different classes. The comparison has to be between two unlike things, such as a leg and an egg, not like a leg and an arm.)

> Fain would I kiss my Julia's dainty leg,
> Which is as white and hairless as an egg. (Robert Herrick)

> O, my love is like a red, red rose,
> That's newly sprung in June.
> O, my love is like the melody,
> That's sweetly played in tune. (Robert Burns)

First, let's assume that the "love" is a woman. The first simile compares her to a "red, red rose," the repetition of "red" intensifying his appreciation of her beauty. She is like a rose "newly sprung in June" suggesting the freshness of her youth. The second simile compares her to the "melody that's sweetly played in tune" suggesting the sweetness and harmony of her personality. She is a joy to see and to hear. If "my love" refers to the speaker's feeling about another person, the first simile compares his feeling of love to "a red, red rose that's newly sprung in June," suggesting the intensity of his love and his excitement at its newness and freshness. The second simile compares his feeling of love to "the melody that's sweetly played in tune"--his being in love gives him a feeling of sweet harmony. Both similes show his happiness as he thinks about his love. In the rest of the poem (not quoted here) he tells his love to the "bonnie lass." If "my love" in the first stanza means his feeling of love, it is his feeling of love for her that he's expressing.

METAPHOR—an implied comparison, without *like* or *as* or *than*.

> All the world's a stage
> And all the men and women merely players;
> And one man in his time plays many parts,
> His acts being seven stages. At first, the infant,
> Mewing and puking in the nurse's arms.

Jacques in Shakespeare's *As You Like It* compares the world to a stage in a theater where human beings are "merely" the acts in a play that goes on for seven acts (seven stages of life). Or each person may play seven roles, all described humorously and cynically by the speaker. Jacques' metaphor presents human life as artificial, monotonous, and all too predictable.

SYMBOL—something that stands for or suggests something else. An image that may suggest multiple meanings. A **conventional** or traditional symbol is an image that is accepted by a culture in general. For example, the cross is a symbol of Christianity; a flag is a symbol for a country.

"Ah Sun-flower" from *Songs of Experience* by William Blake

> Ah, Sun-flower! weary of time,
> Who countest the steps of the Sun,
> Seeking after that sweet golden clime
> Where the traveller's journey is done:
> Where the Youth pined away with desire,

And the pale Virgin shrouded in snow,
Arise from their graves, and aspire
Where my Sun-flower wishes to go.

In "Ah, Sun-flower" by William Blake, the sun-flower is personified—that is, described as human, experiencing human emotions. The sun-flower as a symbol suggests first a weariness with this world and the confines of time; it suggests a frustration at the slowness of life; it suggests longing for fulfillment; it suggests desire for another realm, "the sweet golden clime." The sun is the object of the sun-flower's longing. As a symbol it suggests time moving toward eternity; it suggests completion, fulfillment; it may suggest God; and the "sweet golden clime," the realm of the sun, sunshine, suggests the spiritual realm, the home of the soul and of God. The "Youth pining away with desire" as a symbol suggests frustration, especially sexual frustration. But perhaps the desire he feels is for a more intense, more spiritual life. The "pale Virgin shrouded in snow" intensifies the frustration of the youth and as a symbol suggests frigidity, coldness, lack of response, death (shrouded). Both arise from their graves (a symbol suggesting their state of spiritual death) and aspire "Where my Sun-flower wishes to go"—that is, the spiritual realm, fulfillment, God. Thus the symbols in the poem suggest a longing for a spiritual relationship or union with God. Another reading of the poem might suggest a longing for a more active life, one in which sexuality was expressed rather than repressed.

In the above analysis the key word is "suggests." And no analysis can exhaust all that a symbol suggests. In a longer and more complex work a symbol might suggest even more multiple meanings. And in some works there might not be any symbols at all.

IRONY

- Verbal irony—words with double meanings, both of which the reader underst ands. The discrepancy between what the words appear to mean on the surface and what they really mean.
- Dramatic irony—a condition in which the audience or readers know things that the characters do not know.
- Situation Irony—a set of circumstances that is the opposite of what we might expect to happen.

The Sound of a Poem

RHYTHM—the pattern of stressed and unstressed syllables.

METER—the systematic measurement of the rhythm in terms of syllables or feet and terms of lines or verses.

FOOT—a unit that consists of a stressed and one or two unstressed syllables or two accented syllables (a spondee).

KINDS OF FEET INCLUDE:

Iambic ('ī-ˌam(b))—two syllables, the second syllable stressed. The most common type in English, iambic most matches the rhythm of everyday speech.

> The **Grizz/** ly **bear/** is **huge/** and **wild;/**
> he **has/** de **voured/** the **in/** fant **child**. (A.E. Housman)

Anapestic ('a-nə-ˌpest)—three syllables, the third syllable stressed.

> The **A syr/** ian came **down/** like the **wolf/** on the **fold/**
> And his **co/** horts were **gleam/** ing in **pur/** ple and **gold**. (Lord Byron)

Trochaic (trō-'kā-ik)—two syllables, first syllable accented.

> **Lon** don/ **bridge** is/ **fall** ing/ **down**.

Dactylic ('dak-təl, -ˌtil)—three syllables, first syllable stressed.

> **Touch** her not/ **scorn** ful ly
> **Think** of her/ **mourn** ful ly.

Spondaic ('spän-ˌdē)—two syllables, both stressed. (Not used for whole poems but for variety in a line)

> **Slow down.**
> **Praise him.**

TERMS THAT DESCRIBE THE NUMBER OF FEET IN A LINE INCLUDE:

> monometer—one
> diameter—two
> trimester—three

tetrameter—four
pentameter—five
hexameter—six
heptameter—seven
octameter—eight

Keep in mind that a good poem almost never completely follows one of the above patterns. A reader is usually hearing two rhythms: the main rhythm the poem is written in, such as iambic pentameter, and the rhythm of the actual poem which will probably contain many variations from iambic.

Other Useful Terms

ALLEGORY—a literary work, especially a narrative, in which a second meaning can be found underneath the surface meaning. The allegory can be thought of as an extended metaphor: characters in an allegory may be personifications of abstract qualities. For example, in the medieval play *Everyman*, Everyman, accompanied by Good Deeds, follows Death at the end of the play. True allegory is author-created; the author sets up the second underlying meaning and gives obvious signals to the reader. Readers can create an allegory out of any work by arbitrarily assigning allegorical meaning to characters and images.

ALLITERATION—repetition of identical consonant sounds and of identical initial sounds in two or more words.

Peter Piper picked a peck of pickled peppers.

The moan of doves in immemorial elms.
And murmuring of innumerable bees. (A. Tennyson)

APOSTROPHE—address to an absent person or to a personified object or abstraction.

O Autumn, laden with fruit, and stained
With the blood of the grape, pass not, but sit
Beneath my shady roof ... (William Blake)

ASSONANCE—repetition of identical vowel sounds.

In there stepped a stately raven of the saintly days of yore.

BLANK VERSE—unrhymed iambic pentameter.

O that/ this too/ too sol/ id flesh/ would melt.

CAESURA—a slight pause in the middle of a line.

When my mother died // I was very young
And my father sold me // while yet my tongue. (William Blake)

FREE VERSE—poetry without a regular metrical pattern, depending more on rhythm than on meter. No rhyme.

HYPERBOLE—overstatement, obvious and extravagant exaggeration.

And I will luve thee still, my dear,
Till a' the seas gang dry. (Robert Burns)

METONYMY—a figure of speech in which the name of one thing is used for another which is closely related to it. "Crown" may be used for "ruler." "In the sweat of thy face shalt thou eat bread" (Gen. 3: 19) ("sweat of thy face" suggests hard work; "bread" suggests food).

PARADOX—a statement which seems to be contradictory or absurd but which may be true on some level after careful examination. "Less is more." "The child is the father of the man." (Wordsworth)

PERSONIFICATION—giving human characteristics to animals, inanimate objects, and abstractions.

For mercy has a human heart,
Pity a human face,
And Love, the human form divine,
And Peace, the human dress. (William Blake)

SONNET—a fourteen line poem in iambic pentameter with a tightly organized structure.

ITALIAN SONNET—first eight lines form a unit called the octave, with a rhyme scheme as follows: abba abba. The last six lines form a unit called the sestet, with a rhyme scheme as follows: cde cde.

ENGLISH SONNET—three quatrains (four lines each) with a concluding couplet (two lines). Rhyme scheme: abab cdcd efef gg.

SYNECDOCHE—a figure of speech in which a part represents the whole or the whole represents the part. "Hired hands" for laborers. "Give us this day our daily bread," bread signifying not just food but all that we need. Closely related to metonymy.

SUGGESTIONS TO CONSIDER WHEN READING A POEM

- Look up any words you do not know in a good dictionary. The failure to understand even one word may lead you to misinterpret a poem.
- Identify the speaker of the poem. What voice or voices do you hear in the poem? Is the speaker addressing another person? What emotions is the speaker expressing?
- Read the poem several times.
- Read the poem out loud. The sound of a poem is part of its form.
- Make sure you can follow the syntax of the poem. Poems, like all writings, are composed of sentences. The sentences in poetry are broken up by lines, but one needs to read by sentences as well as by lines.
- Notice the images, similes, and metaphors in the poem. How do the images from one line work with images of other lines?
- Notice the structure of the poem. All poems are constructed in lines. Many poems are divided into stanzas.

QUESTIONS TO CONSIDER WHEN ANALYZING A POEM

- Who is the speaker of the poem? (Remember that the author is not the speaker.) What does the speaker tell us about her or his life, attitudes, emotions, opinions? If you think of the speaker as a character, what kind of person is the speaker? Is the speaker addressing another person?
- How do the images, the metaphors, the similes, the symbols, and other poetic devices work in the poem? How do they contribute to the unity of the poem? How do the parts of the poem relate to each other? Consider how the rhythm of the poem contributes to the whole.
- What conflicts, tensions, and opposites are there in the poem, and how are they resolved by the end of the poem?
- Examine the use of irony, paradox, and ambiguity in the poem. Does the poet ironically suggest the limitations of the speaker at times?

Don't try to turn all poems into allegories. In interpreting a poem, stick as closely as possible to the poem itself, analyzing its images, metaphors, similes, structure, and rhythm. Don't force a moral or an abstract generalization on a poem.

ANALYSIS OF A POEM—AN EXAMPLE

"The Chimney Sweeper" from *Songs of Innocence* by William Blake

When my mother died I was very young,
And my father sold me while yet my tongue,
Could scarcely cry 'weep 'weep 'weep.
So your chimneys I sweep and in soot I sleep.

There's little Tom Dacre, who cried when his head
That curled like a lamb's back, was shaved, so I said,
"Hush, Tom, never mind it, for when your head's bare,
You know that the soot cannot spoil your white hair."

And so he was quiet, and that very night,
As Tom was a sleeping he had such a sight,
That thousands of sweepers, Dick, Joe, Ned, and Jack
Were all of them locked up in coffins of black,

And by came an Angel who had a bright key,
And he opened the coffins and set them all free.
Then down a green plain leaping laughing they run
And wash in a river and shine in the sun.

Then naked and white, all their bags left behind,
They rise upon clouds, and sport in the wind.
And the Angel told Tom, if he'd be a good boy,
He'd have God for his father and never want joy.

And so Tom awoke and we rose in the dark
And got with our bags and our brushes to work.
Tho' the morning was cold, Tom was happy and warm.
So if all do their duty, they need not fear harm.

Innocence in Soot

The speaker of William Blake's "The Chimney Sweeper" is a little boy who was forced to become a chimney sweeper when he was a small child. His attitude toward life, however, is basically cheerful, despite his statement that his mother died when he was very young and that his father sold him before he could even say "sweep" clearly. He is an orphan, alone and unprotected. In the second stanza he tries to cheer up another little boy, Tom Dacre, who is crying because his head has just been shaved as a first step in becoming a chimney sweeper. Seemingly as a result of the speaker's encouraging words, Tom has a dream that gives him a revived outlook on life. He has evidently told the speaker his dream, and the speaker's own hopeful outlook seems to have been strengthened by his response to Tom's dream.

The last line of the first stanza, "Your chimneys I sweep," suggests that the speaker is addressing a customer, a lady or gentleman who probably has asked the little boy to tell something about himself. The boy is too innocent himself to understand that the probably nice person is hiring a small child to do a dirty job. Behind the speaker one can sense the author presenting to the reader a picture of child exploitation (and maybe the reader has hired a chimney sweeper or used children for hard labor).

In the first stanza the speaker says that he was "sold" by his father. The word "sold" suggests that his life is a type of slavery and suggests he feels some bitterness toward his father who abandoned him shortly after his mother's death. He was sold before he could clearly say "sweep." The word he actually says, with unconscious dramatic irony, is "weep," another indication of the misery of the life he leads. The simple word "so" is the word the boy uses to show the reason he sweeps "your chimney" and sleeps in soot. The boy works in and sleeps in dirt.

In the second stanza the speaker uses the simile "curled like a lamb's back" to describe Tom's hair. A lamb is a traditional symbol of innocence, and the comparison of the mutilation of the boy's shaving to a lamb's shearing shows the violation of Tom's innocence by exploiting adults. There is also a contrast between "soot" and "white hair"—black dirt and the white, blond hair of a small child. The whiteness surely suggests innocence that is being contaminated by the dirt of the world. (The white hair might also suggest premature age as the boy is being forced into the world of experience before he is ready for it.) There is some unintentional irony (on the part of the speaker) in the line, "You know that the soot cannot spoil your white hair," for Tom no longer has any hair, and his head is going to be covered with soot in any case.

In the third stanza the speaker begins to narrate Tom's dream. He sees thousands of sweepers with everyday names "locked up in coffins of black." The black coffins suggest the sooty chimneys the boys work in and are a symbol of the death-in-life existence of chimney sweepers.

In the fourth stanza an angel with a bright key releases the boys. The slaves are set free. The angel, a creature of light, and the bright key contrast to the soot of the earlier stanzas. We have an image of a "green plain"; we see the boys leading a natural life, playing instead of toiling. The verbs "leaping," "laughing," "run," "wash," and "shine" suggest an active, natural, spontaneous life. Washing in the river suggests cleansing from the dirt, a kind of baptism into a new life. "Shine in the sun" is another image of light in contrast to darkness. In the fifth stanza we see the boys, "naked and white," cleansed from dirt and given a new or restored innocence. They are free from their sweepers' bags and can rise upon clouds and sport in the wind." They experience a sense of release as they are freed from slavery and death. The main emphasis is on the boys' playing and enjoying life. Here surely the author (working behind the speaker) is presenting a kind of life children ought to be experiencing in this world. It is ironic that the chimney sweepers can only dream of running and playing in some supernatural setting.

The angel then tells Tom that if he's a good boy, "he'd have God for his father and never want joy." It's possible that the boys think of these words as a promise of a future life, of heaven, but the words suggest that Tom can have God for a father and he can have joy now. The angel's words promise God's presence and joy in the boys' present life in this world.

In the last stanza the boys go with their bags (left behind in the dream) and brushes back to work. But even in the "cold," "dark" morning, Tom is "happy and warm." The dream has restored his innocence and given him joy and a sense of God's presence in his life as a chimney sweeper. And the speaker in telling of Tom's happiness seems to feel it himself. The speaker who has been abandoned by his father also can have "God for his father and never want joy."

The last line, "So if all do their duty, they need not fear harm," is the speaker's innocent closing words to the person who is probably hiring him to sweep a chimney. Behind the speaker we can hear the author ironically asking, "If all did their duty, would little children be sweeping chimneys?"

If we examine the rhythm of the poem, we will find that the poem is mainly written in anapestic tetrameter, though most lines contain at least one iambic foot. There is enough variety to keep the poem from becoming singsong. The spondee in the third line gives us three "weeps" in a row, stressing the boy's bitterness and misery and even the monotony of his work. The stanzas of the poem about Tom's dream are rhythmically smooth and fast, suggesting the joy Tom feels in his dream and which the speaker also shares. The last line of the poem is slower and somewhat irregular with both the last two words being stressed: "fear harm." The poem with its simple rhyming couplets and childlike rhythm well conveys the almost desperate innocence of the child in a corrupt, soot-laden world.

3

GENRE APPROACH TO FICTION

Fiction may be defined as a form of literature which tells a story about imagined human beings revealed in action. Forms of fiction include: novels, short stories, epics, parables, narrative poems, and dramas. If asked to describe a story we might think first about characters, perhaps the **protagonist** (the chief character in a story) or the **antagonist** (the character who opposes the protagonist) or even the action (the general idea or situation of the story). In the discussion that follows, I will begin my analysis of fiction with an element Aristotle deemed the "very soul" of a work of fiction: plot. After plot I will examine several other elements vital to fiction, namely theme, character, point of view and setting.

PLOTS, PLOTS, PLOTS

Defining Plot

Aristotle, the Greek philosopher who wrote *On the Art of Poetry* in 330 BCE (the first writer known to have written about plot), is responsible for many of our concepts of plot. He defined plot as the "organization of the incidents of the story"; "structural ordering of the incidents"; "artistic ordering of the incidents." E. M. Forster, in *Aspects of the Novel* defined plot as "a narrative of events, the emphasis falling on causality." An example of a story might be: The king died, and the queen died; an example of a story with a plot: The king died, and the queen died of grief. Plot is the working out of the action, step by step (e.g., Oedipus learns of the plague, he tries to find out who caused it, he sends for an oracle from Delphi, he interviews Tiresias, who tells him he himself caused the plague, etc.)

Unity of plot is crucial in fiction. In a tightly organized plot all details contribute to the whole. Everything that happens must grow out of what happens immediately before until we reach the inevitable conclusion. The plot is a chain of events based on cause and effect. As Aristotle stated, "… the plot, which is an imitation of an action, must represent an action that is organically unified, the structural order of the incidents being such that transporting or removing any one of them will dislocate and disorganize the whole. Every part must be necessary, and in its place …"

Though not all stories can be classified into comic and tragic plot categories, most stories do have endings that are more or less satisfactory for the protagonist. A comic plot is one with a happy or satisfactory ending. (A story with a comic plot may or may not necessarily be funny or humorous.) Stories with tragic plots end with death or misfortune for the main character. The climax indicates that the protagonist has fallen from a higher to a lower condition. The protagonist may fail to reach a goal or fail in a quest. Some modern stories do not emphasize plot or have a traditionally structured plot. These stories, plotless stories, emphasize character or mood or idea. A story may end without the conflict being resolved or the ending may be "open-ended."

Parts of a Plot

EXPOSITION—background information that we need to know in order to understand the characters and their situations. The exposition may be given at the beginning or be distributed throughout the story.

INCITING INCIDENT—the beginning: "that which does not itself come after anything else in a necessary sequence, but after which some other thing … does naturally exist or come to pass." (Aristotle) The incident that starts the action going. The conflict begins.

Almost all stories are based on conflict. Some basic types of CONFLICT are:

- Inner conflict in one character (such as confused or divided motivation, conflict of conscience and ambition, or self-disgust conflicting with pride).
- Conflict of one character with another character (many variations).
- Conflict of a character with an outside force or influence, such as society, nature, the environment, God, fate, etc.

It always helps in analyzing a story to study the conflicts in the story. Such an analysis leads to an understanding of theme.

RISING ACTION—the chain of events from the inciting incident to the climax.

CLIMAX—the turning point to good or bad. The moment of highest tension. Frequently a decision made by the main character which changes her or his life. Finding the climax is usually easy since the whole story is building up to it. The climax is the chief element of the structure of the story, and analyzing its significance leads to an understanding of the theme of the story.

A novel is a long work of fiction which may have a story climax somewhere after the middle; though in any work of fiction the climax may be delayed until the end. Since a novel is made up of episodes, each episode may have its own plot structure.

Plays generally reach their climaxes in the middle. For example, Shakespeare's plays usually have a climax in the third act (of a five-act play). In a short story, the climax usually comes at the end of the story. The falling action and resolution may be done quickly or omitted.

There may be more than one climax in a work of fiction. In some stories one incident may be a turning point that leads to a stronger and more complete turning point later in the story. There may be a separate climax for each major character but most fictions are structured around one strong climax.

FALLING ACTION—the chain of events from the climax to the resolution.

RESOLUTION or DENOUEMENT or UNRAVELING—the plot has reached its conclusion. The conflict is settled. The end.

Plot Analysis of Two Parables

In the fifteenth chapter of Luke, Jesus tells three related parables about the joy of finding lost things: a lost sheep, a lost coin, and a lost son. Let us look at the second story. (The translations come from *The Revised English Bible*.)

Luke 15: 8-10 THE LOST COIN

Or again, if a woman has ten silver coins and loses one of them, does she not light the lamp, sweep out the house, and look in every corner till she has finds it? And when she does, she calls her friends and neighbors together and says, "Rejoice with me! I have found the coin that I lost." In the same way, I tell you, there is joy among the angels of God over one sinner who repents.

This story is very short, but it has a well-structured plot. The inciting incident sets up the conflict: the woman has lost a silver piece. The conflict is her unhappiness and distress at its loss. The rising action is her looking for the coin—she lights the lamp, sweeps the house, and searches the house thoroughly. The climax is finding the coin. This is a turning point for her, a moment of intense emotion, and finding the coin provides a happy ending. One could say that the story ends with the climax, but one might consider her sharing the good news with neighbors as the falling action and resolution.

Luke 15:11-24 THE LOST SON

There was once a man who had two sons; and the younger said to his father, "Father, give me my share of the property." So he divided his estate between them. A few days later the younger son turned the whole of his share into cash and left home for a distant country, where he squandered it in dissolute living. He had spent it all, when a severe famine fell upon the country and he began to be in need. So he went and attached himself to one of the local landowners, who sent him on to his farm to mind the pigs. He would have been glad to fill his belly with the pods that the pigs were eating, but no one gave him anything. Then he came to his senses: "How many of my father's hired servants have more food than they can eat, and here am I, starving to death! I will go at once to my father, and say to him, Father, I have sinned against God and against you; I am no longer fit to be called your son; treat me as one of your hired servants." So he set out for his father's house. But while he was a long way off his father saw him, and his heart went out to him; he came to meet him, flung his arms round him, and kissed him. The son said, "Father, I have sinned against God and against you; I am no longer fit to be called your son." But the father said to his servants, "Quick! fetch a robe, the best we have, and put it on him; put a ring on his finger and sandals on his feet. Bring the fatted calf and kill it, and let us celebrate with a feast. For this son of mine was dead and has come back to life; he was lost and is found. And the festivities began.

In this story the son seems to have a conflict with his father whom he leaves to lead his own independent life of carefree pleasure. He perhaps also has a conflict with society when he finds himself poor and hungry. His greatest conflict, however, is his conflict with himself. Seeking pleasure, he makes a mess of his life and falls into self-pity. The first turning point occurs when "he came to his senses" and resolves to return to his father. He has repented his wasteful life and is willing to work as a servant for his father. But until he receives his father's forgiveness, he is nervous about the outcome—as is the reader. The climax of the story occurs when the father forgives him. The moment of the climax is simply stated: "his heart went out to him." Then we see the father running to the son who makes his prepared confession which the father in his joy doesn't even seem to hear. One might say the falling action and resolution are the father's celebrating the son's return. He dresses his son in his own robe and gives him a ring and a feast—all of these actions make the young man feel that he is again accepted as his father's son.

However, the story is not over. The father has another son who is not at all happy with his father's generous treatment of his brother.

Luke 15:25-32 ANOTHER LOST SON

Now the elder son was out on the farm: and on his way back as he approached the house, he heard music and dancing. He called one of the servants and asked what it meant. The servant told him, "Your brother has come home, and your father has killed the fatted calf because he has him back safe and sound." But he was angry and refused to go in. His father came out and pleaded with him; but he retorted, "You know how I have slaved for you all these years; I never once disobeyed your orders; and you never gave me so much as a kid, to celebrate with my friends. But now that this son of yours turns up, after running through your money with his women, you kill the fatted calf for him." "My boy," said the father," you are always with me, and everything I have is yours. How could we fail to celebrate this happy day? Your brother here was dead and has come back to life; he was lost and has been found."

Here the conflict is brother against brother. It is even more obviously son against father as the elder son reproaches his father for forgiving the younger son. It is also an inner conflict as the elder brother feels self-pity and resentment. In this story the conflict is not resolved. The father tries to make the elder son understand his joy at recovering his lost son, but the story ends without a response from the elder son. Thus the story stops before the climax—it is open-ended. Jesus doesn't even point out the moral here as he usually does in his parables. But isn't this a more effective ending than a definite resolution? We are left with the contrast of two brothers: one who has made a definite change in his life and has learned the values of love— and one who is selfish and resentful and concerned primarily with materialistic values. And the story emphasizes the loving father who not only forgives and welcomes his lost son but reasons lovingly with the other one.

THEME

Finding the Theme

The theme is the controlling idea of the story, the central and unifying concept of the story. The theme is expressed in the entirety of the story—it is not just a moral tacked on at the end. By analyzing how the parts of the story relate to each other and to the whole, we can perceive the theme of the story.

In analyzing the structure of the story of the lost sons, we came to an understanding of the main theme: the value of love and compassion as contrasted to the elder son's materialistic attitude toward life. Another related theme is the joy of finding the lost, a theme that is also reflected in the two other stories Jesus tells here. The father feels joy at finding the lost son; the younger son feels joy at finding the father, and perhaps even more, himself. The older son feels no joy at the return of his brother; his lack of joy indicates his lost self.

The more complex the story, the more complex is the theme—but a careful analysis of the story will help us to put into words what the whole is working to achieve. The way the story is put together, its characterization and point of view, its style and its imagery add up to the meaning to the story.

After finishing a story, ask yourself the significance of the title. The title may be a guide to the theme of the story.

Moral Approach to Literature

Sometimes people ask what the moral of the story is. But a story is not a sermon and very rarely can one sum up a good story with a simple moral. However, stories can be approached from a moral standpoint. We can look at the decisions characters make and judge these decisions. In the story of the lost sons, we see first the decision of the younger son to devote himself to a life of sensual pleasure. The result is poverty and starvation and the sense that the son has lost his true self. His second decision, when he comes to his senses, is to return to his father and begin a new life. The father chooses to forgive him (perhaps "chooses" is too strong a word for the father's spontaneous action). Here the story emphasizes compassion and love. The elder son chooses to be selfish and unbrotherly, and the story suggests that his materialistic attitude limits him as a human being.

The whole structure of a story may lead us to consider certain moral issues and to consider complex questions of right and wrong.

Sometimes in a story we learn with the characters as they struggle to understand themselves and their society. Sometimes we are forced by the structure of the story to understand more than the characters come to understand themselves. We see the characters' mistakes and failures and distorted attitudes toward life.

Social Approach to Literature

The theme of a story may be a character's conflict with society, and the story may be a criticism of society. The story may emphasize characters' struggles against society which represses them as individuals and puts pressure on them to conform to what society expects. Individuals may feel this pressure limits or even destroys their development as whole persons. The story may show how society is unjust, corrupt, inhibiting, or materialistic.

On the other hand, a story may emphasize the immaturity of characters who are rebelling against their society's norms and conventions. The story may focus on the limitations of the characters who have not learned to adjust to their society rather than on the flaws of their society.

Not all stories put an emphasis on society, but most stories show to some extent the effect of society on the character. Even in the story of the lost sons, the elder brother's speech shows that he lives in a society which demands a mechanical devotion to duty: "... I have slaved for you all these years; I never once disobeyed your orders," he says to the father. In trying to live up to what he thinks society expects, he has become an unhappy, unsatisfied person.

CHARACTER

Creating Characters

Aristotle refers to characters as the agents that carry out the action. Thus, a plot consists of the action of the characters. How does a writer create characters that Aristotle requires to be "true to life"?

Fiction by words creates the illusion of living human beings. We know that these characters are creations of the author and that these characters are not flesh and blood (they are composed of words); but successful authors make us believe in the reality of these characters. They make us see them as representative human beings, like us and like people we know.

All characters in fiction are simpler than people in real life, but a successful author makes the characters seem real by giving us a concrete depiction of the way the characters speak, think, appear, and behave, by revealing them as complex human beings, and by showing them following a consistent pattern of personality (each person being inconsistent in his own way). As Aristotle says, characters must be "true to their own nature" throughout the work.

Kinds of Characters

FLAT—"constructed around a single idea or quality." ("Flat" and "Round" character definitions derived from E.M. Forster's *Aspects of the Novel*.) Usually dominated by a single trait: easily recognized when they enter, usually humorous. (No one in real life is a flat character, but we frequently think of people as "flat.") Usually seen from the outside.

ROUND OR COMPLEX—cannot be summed up in a single phrase; change as the story progresses. Three-dimensional characters. Usually seen from the inside.

CHARACTERS IN CLASSICAL AND MODERN LITERATURE— Classical literature puts an emphasis on universal types of characters. Characters, even major and fairly complex ones, are meant to express some basic human characteristics. For example, Odysseus in *The Iliad* is a type of rational man who always keeps his head in a crisis. Aristotle says that poetry (fiction) is superior to history because history expresses the particular and what has happened, while poetry expresses the universal and what may happen. That is, fiction is concerned with what is basic and true of humanity in all periods. Conversely, modern literature usually puts an emphasis on individualized characters rather than on general types.

POINT OF VIEW (OR FOCUS OF NARRATION)

Point of view means the angle from which a story is told. Who is telling the story? On which character or characters does the story focus? Whose minds do we enter, if any?

The Narrator

The **narrator** is the person the author uses to tell the story. Basically there are two types of narrators. First there is the narrator who is a character in the story. This narrator uses the first person (I) and tells the entire story (see "I" under Types of Points of View below).

The second type of narrator is not a character in the story. This narrator may write entirely in the third person but may at times use "I" and offer some comment on the story she or he is telling. This narrator may tell the story by giving us only the external actions and words of the characters and a description of the setting; the narrator may limit the focus to one character and observe that "central intelligence" from both the outside and the inside; the narrator may broaden the focus to two or more characters. But in all of these the second type of narrator presents the characters and actions in a particular way, in a particular style, even with a particular bias. Very much like the narrator who is a character in the story, the narrator who is not a character encloses the story she or he tells with her or his personality, understanding, and consciousness.

Usually one refers to the second type of narrator as "the author," but it is better to think of the narrator as separate from the author—a fictional self through whom the author tells the story. Wayne C. Booth in *The Rhetoric of Fiction* writes: "Even the novel in which no narrator is dramatized creates an implicit picture of an author who stands behind the scene, whether as stage manager, as puppeteer, or as an indifferent God, silently paring his fingernails. This implied author is always distant from the 'real man'—whatever we may take him to be—who creates a superior version of himself, a 'second self,' as he creates his work..." (151).

Booth also thinks we should question the reliability of the narrator, especially in fictions in which the narrator is a character but also in fictions with a narrator who is not a character. Questions of reliability also apply to the characters whose minds we follow in stories told from the omniscient point of view or stories limited to following the point of view of just one character. A narrator is reliable, he says, "when he speaks for or acts in accordance with the norms of the work (which is to say the implied author's norms), unreliable when he does not" (158-159). For example, a story may be told by a narrator who is obviously bigoted, dishonest, and self-seeking. We soon detect behind the story the author's rejection of this character's norms or standards, and we judge the character to be unreliable, both in fact and in ethical standards. If we judge the narrator to be unreliable, we read the story with a certain irony—we read with possibly greater understanding of the story than the narrator has. We can usually identify the narrator whose norms are the same as the author's. We determine a reliable narrator as one whose understanding and evaluation of the characters and actions seem by the end of the story to be right to us; the narrator's norms and values match what the whole story (its structure, the effect it has on us, its style) is saying. However, since no one is perfect, no narrator is absolutely reliable. We tend to trust narrators who are aware of their own limitations more than narrators who have no doubts about the accuracy of their narration. Keep in mind that a "reliable" narrator means more than presenting the facts of the story truthfully; a "reliable" narrator is one whose understanding of the story we can accept and trust.

There are many different ways narrators can present their stories in time. A narrator may tell a story chronologically, beginning with the inciting incident and ending with the incident that happens last. A narrator may structure a story by moving back and forth between two or more different times. The narrator can at any time tell us something about a character's past or give us a glimpse of the character's future.

Generally we think of the second type of narrator, the narrator who is not a character in the story, as male or female depending on the sex of the author. But did Mary Ann Evans using the pen name of George Eliot intend for her readers to consider the narrator of her novels as male? Do we, reading her novels now, think of the narrator as a woman? How does thinking of a narrator as belonging to a particular sex affect our reading of a story?

Types of Points of View

First-person (I) Narration By a Character In The Story

The first-person narrator (using the first person, I or me) may be the main character of the story, or the narrator may be reporting to us his or her observations of other characters. In some stories the narrator may not be involved in the action at all but seemingly giving us an objective account of incidents and people she or he has observed. Yet, whether the narrator is telling a personal story or a story about others, we are interested in the reactions and understanding of the narrator.

The narrator can tell his or her thoughts, reflections, and inner conflicts. The narrator can tell us his or her dreams and in other ways reveal the unconscious. But the narrator is limited, as we all are, in how much understanding of our unconscious motivation we can achieve.

The narrator is, of course, limited to her or his own observation of others. The narrator cannot enter into any other character's mind. The narrator may tell us what other characters have told him or her and may guess the motivations of other characters, but primarily the narrator relates what he or she has seen, heard, and thought. The narrator is limited also by the opportunities he or she has to observe or to participate in the action.

The narrators are also limited by their degrees of intelligence, by their levels of maturity, by their experience in the world, and by many other aspects of their personalities. Authors can achieve very different effects by choosing stupid, naive, and dishonest narrators or bright, perceptive, worldly-wise narrators. Authors, however, will expect their readers to see the limitations of the narrators and to judge the narrators' reliability.

As in any point of view, we always have to question the reliability of the narrator. Does the narrator seem basically honest and direct? Or is the narrator self-deceived? Does the narrator distort the situation because of his or her own emotional involvement in the story?

One effect of the first-person point of view is that it actively involves us in the story, and to some extent it makes us identify ourselves with the narrator. At least we are drawn close to the narrator. But as we read the story, we may question the reliability of the narrator, and by the end of the story, we may reject or doubt the narrator's understanding of what has happened in the story.

Always make a distinction between the author and the narrator. The author uses the narrator to tell the story, but the writer wants us to make up our minds about the narrator, to see her or him as a character in the story.

Another thing to consider about the first-person narrator is the time that has lapsed between the action and the narration. The narrator may be mainly trying to give us a sense of exactly how she or he felt when the story happened, or the narrator may be telling the story as an older, wiser person whose understanding of the story came some time later. Narrators frequently try to do both: to give the reader an understanding of how they felt at the time along with their later, more mature insight. Moreover, there may be a difference between the mature narrator telling the story and the narrator as a character in the story.

First-person narration is a convention of fiction, a method an author uses to tell a story, and the reader accepts a number of variations in the telling which may not really be quite believable. For example, do you believe that Huckleberry Finn would really sit down and write a three-hundred page book? Some first-person narrations seem like autobiographical reflections; some seem to be an oral rather than a written narration, as if the narrator were telling his or her story to a listening audience; some seem to exist only in the minds of the narrators themselves—the reader just happens to be listening to the thoughts of the characters. First person narrators also usually possess the ability to remember the exact words the characters spoke.

Dramatic

The narrator limits the story as in a play to the external actions and words of the characters and to the external settings. The narrator does not enter the mind of even one character. One can think of the narrator as a kind of video camera, recording the setting, the words and actions of the characters, but viewing them only from the outside. Although very few stories are written entirely from this point of view, almost all stories have sections which are composed of dialogue and description. As in drama we learn about characters by their words and actions. We judge them as we do people in real life by external observation. We can only guess their motivations and inner life by what we see. The narrator seems to be a reporter who objectively relates the story. However, the style of the narrator influences the way we respond to the story.

Very few modern stories are told entirely from the dramatic point of view. But folk tales and myths and other stories originally told orally frequently are dramatic in form. (The oral storytellers can give hints of the inner life of characters by gestures and the sound of their voices.)

And keep in mind that almost all stories include the dramatic point of view. The largest part of many stories consists of dialogue plus description.

Limited Omniscience—Focus on One Character—Inside and Outside

This point of view is limited to one character (or central consciousness or intelligence); the narrator tells the story in the third person—he, she. The narrator presents the character both from the outside and the inside. As in a motion picture in which the camera follows only one character, we see the character as the narrator cannot, from the outside. But the narrator can also probe the inner self. In this point of view the narrator is both like a camera and like a god, revealing the inner life of a character in a way that no real human being can do for another person. The narrator may give us the actual words the characters are thinking: we may learn of their emotions and feelings and general states of mind which may not consist of words; we may even go into their subconscious by the narration of dreams and other devices. The narrator can analyze the character and understand her or him more completely and objectively than the character can. This method has some of the characteristics of first-person narration—we focus on one character and to some extent identify with that character. And since we are limited to that one character, one observer or reflector, we have to question his or her reliability in understanding the action and other characters and even the understanding the character has of himself or herself. We have to judge the other characters as they are presented dramatically (dialogue and actions) and determine the bias of the central character. (See comments on reliable narrator above). The degree to which the narrator will explain or comment on the character will vary from one story to another.

A modern version of this point of view is the **stream of consciousness** method, in which the author tries to convey as completely as possible the flow, the stream of thoughts, emotions, and sensory perceptions of a character at the moment the character experiences them. The writer attempts to capture not just the words that may be going through a character's mind but also what the character is seeing, hearing, smelling, tasting, feeling, and the emotions and thoughts that may be just below the conscious level but which keep popping up into consciousness, like memories of past events, hopes and plans for the immediate future, momentary regrets and underlying fears. Try examining your own mind for a moment and list all the thoughts and feelings that are going through it while you are reading this sentence. This method is also sometimes called **the interior monologue.**

Omniscient Point of View

Technically, the omniscient point of view differs from the one character, third-person point of view only in that the narrator enters the mind of more than one character, from two to two thousand. The word omniscient means knowing all, but the omniscient narrator is only omniscient in that he or she goes inside the mind of more than one person, something no human being (as far as I know) can do. The narrator can enter the mind of any of the characters, moving from the present to the past, even to the future, going from earth to Olympus, or the other side of the galaxy, but no author can tell all: authors limit themselves, emphasizing a few major characters and a limited action. Omniscient authors, like all authors, must select their material to give a meaningful interpretation of life. (One might say that there are really no omniscient narrators, since no human being can be omniscient and God doesn't write fiction.)

This point of view, like the others, includes the dramatic or objective point of view. It also includes the third-person point of view and may include some first-person accounts, such as diaries and letters. In some chapters of a novel, for example, an author might present only an account of the setting and the dialogue of the characters. In some chapters the author might switch back and forth from the consciousness of one character to another. In other chapters the author might present whole chapters from the point of view of only one character. The advantage of this point of view is a complex view of life and people. We can see the interaction and contrast of characters as we switch from one point of view to another. There is usually an element of dramatic irony, since we the readers know more than any of the characters and understand the whole action better than any individual character. However, omniscient narrators can keep secrets and withhold information from us as well as from the characters.

We can also get a panoramic view of society if the author takes us into the minds of characters from different parts of society.

SETTING

The setting is the time and place of a story. When exactly is a story happening? Almost all stories are narrated in the past tense, but the setting includes information about the period in which the story takes place—perhaps in the American Civil War, or in the contemporary world, or even in the distant future. The time also includes the season of the year and the periods of night and day. The work of fiction may extend for years or emphasize a few hours or even minutes. Regardless of the total extent of time of the narrative (whether ten minutes or fifty years), the dramatized portion of the narrative will focus on particular periods such as June 1, 1979, from 5:00 to 5:30 p.m. (although the exact times will seldom be stated).

The place of the story refers to where the story is happening. A story may be limited to one place, like a room, or may move from one scene to another. Usually the story takes place in a particular nation, in a particular city or town, or some spot in the country, even on a particular planet (if the story is a science-fiction story, perhaps not the earth).

The concept of setting could be extended to include the whole general environment or atmosphere in which the characters live.

Details of the setting may be given in long descriptive passages, or the details can also be distributed throughout the story as we observe the characters in their environment and are given glimpses of the background of their actions. The effect of a concrete setting is to make the story more vivid and realistic to us. The author helps us to visualize the background and to imagine and to see the characters in it.

The setting is a part of the whole story. The setting may reinforce the

theme of the story. A character may be in conflict with his or her environment (plot). The setting may reveal or test the characters. Each separate
point of view will present setting differently. First-person narrators will
present the setting through their own personal biases. Omniscient narrators
may be more objective in describing the backgrounds.

Let us look at the setting in Jesus' story of the lost sons. First we probably observe that the time of the story is contemporary with the telling of
the story, although the story is meant to be universal. The time of the story
includes the day the father divided the property, the years the younger son
squandered his life, the moment he comes to his senses, and the first hour
or so of return. It is the return home that is dramatized and that is the heart
of the story.

Basically there are two places in the story. One is the place of exile,
where the young man (a Jew), finds himself feeding pigs and longing to eat
the pigs' food. The main setting is the father's estate—a place of plenty and
hospitality, of kindness and forgiveness. The effect of the contrast in the
settings, of course, is part of the effect of the whole story.

QUESTIONS TO CONSIDER WHEN ANALYZING FICTION

PLOT: Analyze the structure of the plot. What is the inciting incident
which begins the conflict? What is the climax of the story? What is the
resolution of the story? Are there any incidents or episodes in the story that
do not contribute to the unity of the plot?

What CONFLICTS are there in the story, and how are they resolved? Analyze the inner conflicts of one or more characters, the conflicts among the
characters, and the conflicts the characters have with society, the environment, or some other outside force.

THEME: How do the conflicts and their resolution in the story reveal
the theme, the controlling idea of the story? How do the different parts of
the story work to create the unity of the story, the overall meaning? What
moral choices and decisions do the characters make in the story? What
ethical questions does the story raise, and what conclusions can we reach by
the way these questions and problems are worked out in the story? How is
the story a criticism of society? How do the characters' conflicts with their
society reveal either the characters' immaturity or the shortcomings of their
society?

CHARACTER: Are the characters in the stories "realistic," true to life? Which characters are "flat"? Which characters are "round" or complex? Are the characters universal types or complex individuals?

POINT OF VIEW: Is the NARRATOR a character in the story? If so, consider the following questions: Is the narrator the main character? If not, what part does the narrator play in the action? How intelligent and perceptive is the narrator? How reliable is the narrator? Does the narrator seem basically honest and direct? Does the narrator distort the situation because of his or her involvement in the story? Does the narrator's understanding of the characters and actions seem by the end of the story to be right to you? How much time has lapsed since the story the narrator is telling took place? Does the narrator seem a more mature person than she or he was at the time of the action? How much does the narrator use the dramatic method? Does the dialogue sound authentic?

If the narrator is not a character in the story, consider these questions: Does the narrator, even though not a character in the story, seem to have a definite personality? What values, philosophy or understanding of life, biases does the narrator have?

Does the narrator seem to be reliable? Is the story told at least in part from the DRAMATIC point of view—consisting of dialogue and description of the setting and the actions of the characters? Does the narrator enter the mind of only one person (LIMITED OMNISCIENCE)? How does the narrator present the inside of the person, her or his conscious and unconscious mind? Consider any analysis the narrator makes of the characters' motivation and behavior. How reliable is the understanding of the main character? OMNISCIENT: Does the narrator enter the mind of more than one character? (If so, all the above questions in this paragraph are applicable.) Which characters does the narrator enter? What greater understanding do you the reader have as a result of entering the minds of more than one character?

SETTING: When and where is the story happening? What does the setting contribute to the story? How does it reveal character and develop the plot? If there is more than one setting in a story, how does the contrast of the settings develop the story?

Works Cited

Aristotle. *On the Art of Poetry.* Trans. Lane Cooper. Ithaca: Cornell University, 1947.

Booth, Wayne C. *The Rhetoric of Fiction.* 2nd Ed. Chicago: University of Chicago Press, 1961.

Forster, E.M. *Aspects of the Novel.* New York: Harcourt. Brace, & World, 1927.

The Revised English Bible with the Apocrypha. Oxford University Press and Cambridge University Press, 1989.

4

GENRE APPROACH TO DRAMA

DRAMA AS LITERATURE

From *Hamlet* by William Shakespeare

Barnardo: Who's there?
Francisco: Nay, answer me. Stand and unfold yourself.
Barnardo: Long live the king.
Francisco: Barnardo?
Barnardo: He.
Francisco: You come most carefully upon your hour.
Barnardo: 'Tis now struck twelve. Get thee to bed, Francisco.
Francisco: For this relief much thanks. 'Tis bitter cold, And I am sick at heart.

To see what makes drama a separate form of literature all one has to do is to look at any page of a play and see that the work is constructed primarily of dialogue. We have a character's name followed by a speech she or he makes. And there will be directions usually in italics or parentheses or at least separated from the dialogue telling us what gestures and actions the characters do. There may be other comments by the author introducing us to the characters, describing the physical setting in which the characters are found, and perhaps comments filling us in on the historical or social background. But the heart of the play we read is the words the characters say.

As a literary work any approach we apply to fiction works for drama. A play like any other story may have a plot with a strong climax. It centers on characters, perhaps even more than short stories or novels, in that it consists almost entirely of words and actions of the characters. Its point of view, of course, is what we earlier labeled "dramatic" or "objective," with the story consisting of words and actions of the characters without the author intruding or going inside the minds of the characters. And like any other form of literature we can apply psychological, archetypal, or any other general literary approach to a play. But what really makes a play unique is that it is written to be performed by actors on a stage or other acting areas; and while we may read a play as we might any other piece of fiction, we cannot divorce the play we read from at least imagining the play performed.

DRAMA AS PERFORMANCE

The first plays in Western literature that still survive are the plays of the Greek playwrights, Aeschylus, Sophocles, Euripides, and Aristophanes. Although for centuries these plays have been read, studied and used as models for almost all other plays in our literature, they were originally written to be performed at the annual festival of Dionysus in the theater below the Acropolis in Athens.

The written form of the play originally served as the **script** of a performance that might be used again for other performances, usually with some adaptations. If we consider the written form of the play as a literary work of art, we must consider the performance of the script as a separate work of art. In fact, each performance, and especially each production of a play, is a separate work of art.

A performance of a play requires an audience, and this in itself distinguishes drama from other literary works which are read by individuals, usually privately. Even in reading a play, one needs to take into consideration how the play might be presented to an audience and how the performance of a play might affect an audience.

The creator the script is usually one person, the author, but it takes the collaboration of many people to put on a performance of the script. The person, at least in modern times, chiefly responsible for creating the performance is the director who coordinates all the participants and materials to construct a unified work of art. Most prominent are the actors, but a modern director needs the assistance of stage managers, lighting technicians, scene shifters, costume designers, and many others. Dramatists know that the scripts they write will need to be brought to life by actors in performance.

The very word "performance" suggests the actors impersonate the characters. In reading a play, we particularly notice the words the characters say, but in watching and listening to a play, we notice the actors' facial and bodily gestures, their movements on the stage, the tone, loudness, and variations of their voices, and their general physical appearance. In reading a play we focus just on the character speaking, but in watching a play we observe all the actors on the stage and may focus as much on the characters being spoken to as on the character speaking. How the actors are arranged on the stage is also important.

In writing a play the dramatists will have definite ideas about the characters they are creating, but they know that the actors will create different characters by the way they perform their roles. In one sense a dramatist's conception of a character is always incomplete; it is only when an actor plays the role on the stage that the character becomes fully realized. Even if one writes a role for a particular actor, one knows that the actor will add much to the part that one cannot anticipate. Part of the excitement of writing a play must be the fact that the completed work of art will be done by others, and if the play is successful, it will be done in many different ways.

In reading a play we may be given information about the setting of the stage, the properties used in a scene, the costumes of a character; but when we are watching a play, these things are always in view and form a part of our consciousness.

The length of a work to be read may vary from a few lines or pages to many volumes, but the length of a play depends to some extent on how long an audience can sit at one time without getting restless. Usually, we expect a play to last no longer than two or three hours.

Almost all plays are constructed chronologically so that each scene follows in time the scene before it. The play seems to happen as we watch it. We are always in the present tense, or as Thorton Wilder says, "The action on the stage takes place in a perpetual present time." (There are some experimental plays which include flashbacks, comments on the past and future by a narrator, and other time-disturbing devices, but most plays are presented straightforwardly with no interruptions in time or from outside the characters, such as a narrator. Wilder's *Our Town* is one of the plays that doesn't follow these usual conventions.)

Because the characters are presented to us directly on the stage, the author cannot take us inside the characters' minds. Instead, we learn about the inner life of characters in much the same way we learn about people in real life: we guess the inner thoughts and feelings and motivations of characters by their words and actions. We see them react to other characters and reveal themselves gradually as the play progresses. The dramatic method requires us to make our own judgments based on what we see and hear. However, the play is usually constructed so that we can tell when characters are telling the truth. Sometimes characters have best friends, **confidants**, to whom they can tell their private thoughts. Moreover, plays frequently are based on crises which force characters to examine themselves and reveal themselves more easily to others.

Two other devices used by Shakespeare and other dramatists, even sometimes today, are the soliloquy and the aside. The **soliloquy** is a speech made by an actor alone on the stage. In the **aside** a character steps away from the other characters and says something to the audience not heard by any of the other characters on the stage.

In every age people go to a play knowing what conventions of the theater to expect. Before they even enter into a theater, they have a good idea of how the theater is built, where the audience sits in relation to the stage, and how they are supposed to behave (when to clap, etc.), among other things. The ancient Greeks expected the actors (all men) to wear masks; they expected that a chorus would dance and sing odes between scenes. Shakespeare's audience expected boys to play women's parts; they expected much of the play to be written in iambic pentameter (even if they didn't know the term). When we go to the theater today, we usually expect to see the stage separated from the audience; we expect that the lights will go out on the audience and the stage will then be illuminated; we expect the curtain to rise to begin the play. When the play is over, we applaud, and the actors come out and bow. If we go to a non-traditional theater, we usually know what we are getting into; we expect the usual conventions to be violated in some way. It helps in reading plays to be aware of the conventions of the period in which the play was written.

In reading plays, we need to consider much of the above. We need to imagine a performance of the play and to see ourselves as part of an audience. Although reading a play is a much more limited experience than watching a play, it can be rewarding. To some extent, we can create the play in our heads; at least we speak the words in our minds and can imagine the interaction among the characters.

In addition to the stage play, we can experience drama as performance in films seen in theaters and on television. The first obvious difference is that while we are an audience responding to actors, the actors cannot respond to us; and we lose the excitement and tension of responding to a live performance. But we are still an audience whether we are watching a film in a crowded theater or are watching it alone in our living rooms. Instead of watching the stage where the actors perform, we watch the picture that the camera has created for us—we see what the director and editor of the film want us to see. Films are not limited by what the stage can realistically present or imaginatively suggest; we can go in a moment from a caveman throwing a bone into the air to a space ship moving smoothly to the moon. And a different medium results in different kinds of acting. Partly because of close-ups, we observe closely the facial expressions of the actors; their eyes especially seem to reveal the insides, the souls of the characters.

Films, perhaps more than stage plays, emphasize the visual, but films have an aural aspect that most plays lack—music, which is used to manipulate our emotions. Films too are a collaborative art; notice how long the credits are at the end of recent films. Finally, a film is a work of art that can be watched many times if one wants to; a performance of a play is a work of art that vanishes as it is created.

TRAGEDY

Before Aristotle

Since Aristotle was the first critic to write on tragedy, discussion of tragedy usually starts with his *Poetics*. But Aristotle composed his theories of tragedy after the three great writers of Greek drama had died, having written close to three hundred tragedies, about thirty of which have survived.

Technically, a **tragedy** was a serious play that was presented at a dramatic festival. Most of the surviving plays were presented at the Festival of Dionysus in Athens. Each tragedy was a separate play but also was one part of **trilogy**. The three tragedies in the trilogy might be connected in plot or in theme. Most tragedies were based on mythological stories from the epic tradition, such as stories about the Trojan War.

The characters, both male and female, are usually of heroic, larger-than-life stature, although the characters in Euripides' plays were more realistic. At the same time, the characters probably resembled to some extent contemporary Athenians, the people in the audience. Each play is fairly short, lasting about an hour and half or less in performance. Perhaps because of its limited length, a play usually consists of one action taking place in a short period of time in one setting. These are serious plays, concerned with moral and religious themes. The characters confront each other, Fate, and the gods. But these plays do not always end unhappily. In Aeschylus' *The Eumenides*, Orestes, after having killed his mother in the second play of the trilogy, is found not guilty and goes home. The protagonist of a tragedy, even when defeated may not die; Oedipus blinds himself and demands to be sent into exile, but he does not die. (His death in *Oedipus at Colonos* is more of a holy transformation and victory than the "tragic" death Shakespeare's heroes experience.)

Each Greek play was performed without intermission, but we can divide it into parts. The play begins with a prologue, which consists of dialogue between one to three characters or sometimes a soliloquy. Next comes the formal entrance of the chorus who chant an ode and dance. The rest of the play consists of episodes, in which the characters talk to each other and to the chorus leader (also a character) followed by chorus odes in which the chorus of twelve sing an ode in unison and dance. Except for a couple of Greek plays, the chorus does not leave the orchestra until the play ends. The chorus usually represent the community where the play is taking place; what happens to the ruler affects all the people. In each of the Greek plays, the chorus has a different personality and plays a different part in the action.

The plays were presented at an outdoor theater with the actors wearing masks.

Aristotle on Tragedy

While realizing the great variety of plays presented in the Greek theater, Aristotle has his own concept of the ideal tragedy—a concept that has since influenced many writers of tragedy and even more critics. It is not always easy to know exactly what Aristotle meant, but perhaps that's not finally important in understanding tragedy. Aristotle's ideas or our ideas of Aristotle's ideas are helpful in understanding the idea of tragedy—from Aeschylus to Arthur Miller. In an early section in *The Poetics*, Aristotle states that the agents of tragedy "must be represented as better than we ourselves." It is the "nobility of the agents" that distinguishes tragedy from comedy. By "better" Aristotle seems to mean "goodness"—the tragic person is better morally than other people. In Chapter 12 Aristotle also says that the tragic hero must be "highly renowned and prosperous." And in Chapter 12, before Aristotle presents his idea of the most effective kind of tragic protagonist, he gives three types of plots that should be avoided, each centering on characters who fail to move us emotionally. First is the fall of good and just persons from happiness to misery. Second is the rise of evil people from ill fortune to prosperity. And third is the downfall of the utter villain. None of these characters arouse pity or fear.

The truly tragic protagonist must arouse pity and fear in us, the audience (or readers). Aristotle says **pity** is "what we feel at a misfortune that is out of proportion to the faults of a man." One suffers more than one deserves. For example, Jason in Euripides' *Medea*, who has abandoned his wife for a younger woman, surely does not deserve to have his children murdered by their mother. We feel pity for the character who has suffered intensely and perhaps somewhat unfairly. This pity is closely associated with **fear**—fear is what we feel when misfortune comes upon one like ourselves. Our pity for the one who has suffered more than he or she deserves becomes fear when we think the same thing may happen to us in similar circumstances. Perhaps Aristotle is suggesting our identification with the tragic protagonists. We identify with them in their undeserved sufferings.

Thus, tragic protagonists cannot arouse pity or fear if they are excessively good or evil. The tragic protagonist must be one "intermediate between these extremes"—not one who is perfectly good or just, nor one "whose misfortune comes about through vice and depravity."

Instead, the downfall of the tragic protagonist must come about "through some error or shortcoming." The Greek word is *hamartia*, which Lane Cooper suggests emphasizes "the lack of insight within a man" and also "the outward fault resulting from" the lack of insight. Sometimes *hamartia* is translated as **the tragic flaw**—some weakness or fault in a person that leads to disaster. Or hamartia may refer to the error that the protagonist makes that leads to a downfall. However we interpret this word, we can see that Aristotle is suggesting that the tragic individual is responsible to some extent for his or her own fall. One may suffer more than one deserves, but one has caused that suffering oneself. The structure of a perfect tragedy thus is one in which the main character changes from prosperity to a fall. There is a **reversal of situation** (*peripeteia*) from good to bad fortune.

One thing Aristotle does not discuss is the part of the gods in bringing about the downfall of the heroes. However, if the heroes suffer more than they deserve, perhaps it is the gods who are punishing them or who are working behind the scenes to carry out divine justice. Heroes, seeking to fulfill their own desires, commit acts that defy or anger the gods—commit hubris (which basically means violence but is usually defined as pride that leads the character to rebel against the gods), and, as a result, are destroyed by the gods. Or one may see the heroes as having disrupted the natural order and in the process causing extreme suffering to themselves.

Aristotle's pattern for the perfect tragedy does not really fit many plays. It does fit Sophocles' *Oedipus Tyrannos* and Shakespeare's great tragedies. Even the Greeks themselves had many excellent plays with other kinds of protagonists and actions. Because a play does not match Aristotle's definition of an ideal tragedy does not mean it is not a good play or even a good tragedy.

Shakespeare's Tragedies

The world's greatest writer of tragedy is generally considered to be the English playwright William Shakespeare (1564-1616). Although Shakespeare did not seem to know the Greek dramatists or Aristotle directly, his plays, like all plays of Western civilization, were greatly influenced by the Greeks. His tragedies all follow Aristotle's basic specifications for an ideal tragedy: they center on the downfall of a hero.

However, Shakespeare's London audiences, of course, came with different expectations of tragedy than did the Greeks. They expected the plays to last longer—from two to three hours. Shakespeare's plays, divided into five acts by the editors but probably presented without intermission, present characters that may change and develop in a complex plot. Audiences knew they were watching a tragedy when they saw the stage draped in black, and they knew that the tragedy would end in the death of the main character. *The Tragedy of Hamlet Prince of Denmark* could only end with the death of Hamlet.

Shakespeare's theater was a building with a stage under the open sky. Although there might have been two thousand people attending a performance at the Globe, all the audience was fairly close to the stage. A company of professional actors performed the plays in repertoire, with boys playing the female characters.

Any discussion of tragedy will emphasize Shakespeare's greatest achievement: his four great tragedies, each of which presents a very different kind of tragic protagonist: Hamlet, the idealist in an imperfect world, struggling with questions of identity and the meaning of life as he tries to force himself to avenge his father's death; Othello, the noble general, tempted by Iago to see his wife and himself as evil; Macbeth, the ambitious man who kills the king to become the king and becomes increasingly evil in the process; King Lear, the old king who gives his kingdom away and learns to value love as he is plunged into a world of suffering. Each play reveals Shakespeare's deep understanding of the tragic concept of life.

The Concept of the Tragic

The tragic concept of life, perhaps best expressed in Shakespeare, can be found in other works of literature besides drama. One of the earliest tragic characters is Achilles in Homer's *Iliad*, who, shamed by Agamemnon, withdraws from fighting and questions the meaning of life:

Fate is the same for the man, the same if he fights hard.
We are all held in a single honour, the brave with the weaklings.
A man dies still if he has done nothing, as one who has done much.
(IX 317-320)

The tragic concept begins with confronting death, feeling the transitory nature of human existence. The tragic protagonist attempts somehow to go beyond the human limitations, to strive for greater glory or honor or richness of experience than is allotted one by fate or the gods. Arthur Miller says "the tragic feeling is evoked in us when we are in the presence of a character who is ready to lay down his life, if need be, to secure one thing—his sense of personal dignity" (144). The tragic hero sees the wrongs, injustices, and imperfections of the world and endeavors to reach beyond these limitations toward greatness.

In striving to attain a fuller expression of one's own individuality, the tragic hero acts, usually irrationally and always irrevocably, setting in motion a chain of events that leads to his or her destruction. Karl Jaspers expresses this concept thus:

> It is only then, through his own actions, that man enters into the tragic-involvement that inevitably must destroy him. What will be ruined here is not merely man's life as concrete existence, but every concrete embodiment of whatever perfection he sought. (15)

Listen to the chorus in *Oedipus* lament the fall of their great king, who earlier had saved them from the death grip of the Sphinx and who had ruled them wisely and well but who is now revealed as the father-killer and mother-marryer who has polluted the land:

> Bending your bow to the breaking-point
> you captured priceless glory, O dear god,
> and the Sphinx came crashing down ...
> you rose and saved our land.
> From that day on we called you king
> we crowned you with honors, Oedipus,
> towering over all—
> mighty king of the seven gates of Thebes.
> But now to hear your story—is there a man more agonized?
> More wed to pain and frenzy? (233-234)

This is the essence of the tragic fall: a great man stretching his bow to the breaking point in his effort to achieve greatness but destroying himself by that very effort. And yet on another level Oedipus is not destroyed. The play does not end with the chorus' lament; we see Oedipus in the last part of the play accepting responsibility for what has happened but also insisting on his own will. He tells the new ruler to send him into exile for the people's good; he still cares about his people and his innocent, suffering daughters. While the tragic protagonist falls and usually dies, there is a celebration or tragic affirmation of human aspirations. Herbert Muller in *The Spirit of Tragedy* suggests the spiritual triumph of the tragic hero:

> In terms of the tragic rhythm, the hero not only proves equal to the "perception" of his fate, but is a better man for this perception.

Finally he is superior to his fate. The major element in the tragic pleasure the common element in the diverse versions of life expressed in the great tragedies—is a reverence for the human spirit. Man retains his dignity in failure and death, whether or not he is to enjoy a life to come. Because of this dignity, all is not vanity (17).

COMEDY

Comedy, like tragedy, originated with the ancient Greeks. After sitting through three tragedies at the Festival, the audience would see a satyr play—a play that might have been a grotesque fantasy, or a humorous dramatization of a story connected to the tragedies just presented, or perhaps just a less serious play. In the afternoon people could go to a comedy at the same theater. The surviving plays of Aristophanes are truly funny plays which illustrate beautifully some of the characteristics that we still expect to find in comedies.

Comic Characterization

The characters in Aristophanes' comedies are as Aristotle says in his Poetics "worse than in everyday life." Again, by "worse" Aristotle means morally worse. Or we could say that comic characters are less than life-size—exaggerated, simplified, distorted, and frequently ridiculous versions of human beings. Many comic characters are dominated by one trait. They may be angry, gullible, stubborn, or stupid.

They can usually be expected to act in the same way each time they appear, although will usually surprise us by some new twist of their peculiar trait. Comic characters seldom change in the course of the play. We enjoy seeing them remain true to their original comic flaw. Comic characters are also usually indestructible; they may survive all sorts of catastrophes and retain their basic comic personality untouched.

Comic characters are like children in their simple reaction to life. Comic characters could be classified as two kinds of children: the agreeable and the disagreeable—or we could say characters we like and characters we enjoy disliking. The agreeable type is often easily excited, fascinated by the new, eager for new experiences, easily amused by oddities, enthusiastic, naive, spontaneous, sometimes innocent, frequently mischievous. The disagreeable characters are like unhappy, misbehaving children who indulge in temper tantrums, quarrel and become upset easily, feel sorry for themselves, react stubbornly and unpleasantly to adverse situations.

Humor in characterization also spawns contrasts of different types of character: the agreeable and disagreeable child and their many variations, such as the timid, helpless character versus the domineering, aggressive person; the lifeless versus the vivacious; the simple buffoon versus the witty, sophisticated person.

Motivation of comic characters is also childish. Comic characters are at the mercy of their bodies. As Walter Kerr suggests in *Tragedy and Comedy*, human beings, supposedly rational creatures, act irrationally when their bodies demand food, sex, or shelter. Among the most familiar comic images, Kerr says, are: "the hungry man staring at food," "the shabbily dressed man shivering in the doorway," and "the sexually deprived man howling at the moon" (155). (None of these images are, of course, funny in themselves. They are funny in a play because the dramatist exaggerates them and makes us see how ridiculous we are when we are slaves to our own bodies.) Comic characters also may crave money, prestige, social position, and power. To obtain their desires, they may practice cunning in their efforts to outwit the authorities and anyone else that gets in their way.

Looking at comic characters from a Freudian angle (see Chapter 5), we can see them indulging theirs its (ids), satisfying their basic urges without worrying about their above-I's (super-egos). Part of the fun of a comedy is watching the characters indulge themselves and act freely and spontaneously—we vicariously enjoy their breaking the rules of society and getting away with it. The child in us responds to their childlike pleasure and actions. Also, we enjoy watching a character with a severe above-I, an uptight person trying to enforce strict conformity to society's standards on others, made fun of and comically deflated. We can momentarily relax from the pressures of our own above-I's as we watch the fun-loving Tom Sawyer get revenge on his nasty, conforming little brother Sid.

One final observation on characterization in comedy takes us back to the comedies of Aristophanes. Unlike the Greek tragedies whose characters were usually mythological heroes from the epic tradition, the comedies took place in contemporary Athens. The characters were Athenians, comic versions of people one knew in everyday life. Even the gods when they appeared talked and acted like Athenian citizens. Writers of comedy since then have generally created characters who resembled present-day human beings, even if the plays are set in the past.

Structure and Plot in Comedy

There are many definitions of comedy, but surely it is safe to say that when we go to a comedy, we expect to laugh. And once we start laughing and are caught up in the comedy, we feel a spirit of fun, a sense of holiday, a good feeling that whatever crisis develops everything will turn out all right in the end. Part of our pleasure in comedy is our expectation of the happy ending. The plot of the comedy may tease us, confuse us, frustrate us, worry us, but we are always anticipating the exciting happy conclusion of the action.

Unlike the Greek writers of tragedy who took most of their plots from traditional stories, Aristophanes invented his plots from scratch. He started with some problem or crisis and let the play develop from that. In *Lysistrata* some wives frustrated by the absence of their husband in the war of Athens and Sparta go on a sex strike. The plays ends with a truce. The comic plot usually begins with some problem, crisis, complication that has to be resolved before the happy ending can be reached. The situation may get very messy and confused as one complication leads to another, but the greater the tangle, the more fun it is to see it untangled. Comic plots are not strictly realistic; absurd coincidences, improbable turns of fortune, character reversals, surprises of all sorts can be accepted as long as we are kept laughing.

Archetypally, the structure of comedy is death followed by rebirth as spring follows winter—"if winter comes, can spring be far behind?" Knowing that spring is coming helps us to endure the harshness of winter, and anticipating the happy ending of the comedy helps us to laugh at the frustrations and even miseries of the plot—and of life.

QUESTIONS TO CONSIDER WHEN ANALYZING DRAMA

DRAMA AS LITERATURE

- Since a play is a work of fiction, the questions on analyzing fiction can be applied to drama. (See the end of Chapter 3.)

DRAMA AS PERFORMANCE

- How might the play be performed? Consider problems of staging, audience response, and interaction among actors on the stage. Consider the different ways a character might be portrayed by the same actor or by different actors. If you are analyzing a performance of a play, either live or filmed, consider how components of the production (the scenery, the costumes, the style of acting, etc.) contribute to the effect of the whole performance.

- What kind of completed characters do the actors create?
- What methods does the author use to take us inside the characters?

TRAGEDY

If a play has an unhappy ending or is deeply serious, we might apply Aristotle's concept of tragedy to the play:

- Is the hero a highly renowned and prosperous person, someone greater than the average person?
- Is there a tragic situation in which a hero suffers a misfortune, falling from a higher to a lower situation?
- Do we feel pity for the hero who suffers more than she or he deserves?
- Do we feel fear because the misfortune falls on someone like ourselves, someone we can identify with?
- Does the tragic protagonist have a flaw or make a mistake that results in a fall?

Other concepts of the tragic:

- What part does fate or the gods have in the hero's downfall?
- How is the hero striving to go beyond human limitations, striving for greater glory or honor or richness of experience than mortals can usually be expected to achieve?
- Does the hero reach wisdom, deeper understanding of life as the result of suffering?
- Does the play confirm and perhaps celebrate human values?

COMEDY

- How are characters humorous: dominated by one trait, distorted, exaggerated, unchanging, behaving like children? How is their motivation comic? How are they slaves of their bodies? Are they seeking prestige, social position, power?
- How is the plot funny? What comic situation, crisis, complication does the author create, and how is it resolved?
- Archetypally, how does the comedy celebrate spring, new beginnings?

Many plays, especially modern plays, cannot always be classified as comedies or tragedies, though usually a play comes closer to one category than another. Moreover, one can find serious characters and situations in a comedy and humorous characters and episodes in a tragedy. Thus, the questions on comedy and tragedy may overlap.

Works Cited

Aristotle. *On the Art of Poetry*. Trans. Lane Cooper. Revised Ed. Ithaca: Cornell University Press, 1962.

Homer. *The Iliad of Homer*. Trans. Richmond Lattimore. Chicago: The University of Chicago Press, 1951.

Jaspers, Karl. "The Tragic Awareness." Trans. K.W. Deutsch. In Tragedy: *Modern Essays in Criticism*. Ed. Laurence Michel and Richard B. Sewall. Englewood Cliffs: Prentice Hall, 1963.

Kerr, Walter. *Tragedy and Comedy*. New York: Clarion (Simon and Schuster), 1968.

Miller, Arthur. *Death of A Salesman: Text and Criticism*. Ed. Gerald Wales. New York: The Viking Press, 1967.

Muller, Herbert. *The Spirit of Tragedy*. New York: Washington Square Press, 1965.

Sophocles. *The Three Theban Plays*. Trans. Robert Fagles. New York: Penguin, 1984.

5

FREUDIAN APPROACH TO LITERATURE

Sigmund Freud (1856-1939), the founder of modern psychoanalysis, has had a profound influence on modern literature and modern literary criticism. It is especially his emphasis on the unconscious that has stimulated artists and critics. Freud did not claim to have discovered the unconscious. He knew that artists as far back as the time of Homer understood to some extent the role of the unconscious in people's lives.

Freud, who lived and wrote in Vienna, wrote in German. In a recent book, *Freud and Man's Soul*, Bruno Bettelheim has argued very persuasively that Freud's terms have been mistranslated into English, and, as a result, his ideas have been distorted. I have found his analysis very helpful.

CONSCIOUS, UNCONSCIOUS, AND PRECONSCIOUS

Freud did not think that **the conscious** needed to be defined. But we might define it as that part of the mind that is aware of itself and of its immediate environment. It is that part that thinks, feels, remembers, and reacts to the external world.

Freud defines **the unconscious** as a process "whose existence we are obliged to assume—for some such reason as that we infer it from its effects—, but of which we know nothing" (62). In other words, we know that we have an unconscious because we can feel its effects on our lives and behavior, but we are not directly aware of it. It is not directly accessible to us.

The preconscious is the kind of unconscious that is "easily, under frequently occurring circumstances, transformed into something conscious" (63). It is latent and accessible to us. In the other kind of unconscious, "this transformation is difficult and takes place only subject to a considerable expenditure of effort or possibly never at all" (63). Freud labeled this the "unconscious."

THE I, THE IT, AND THE ABOVE-I (EGO, ID, AND SU-PER-EGO)

Freud thought the personality (actually the word Freud used was "Seele"—the German word for "soul") has three aspects or parts. We sometimes talk of them as if they were separate entities, but as Bettelheim points out, "they cannot be separated from each other except in theory. Each of them, in its own way, exercises an important and different—albeit overlapping—function in the psyche" (58).

The I (Ego)

The usual English translation of the term Freud uses for the conscious self is "the ego," but, as Bettelheim stresses, in the original German Freud uses "das Ich," the simple word for "I." Bettelheim states that what Freud calls the I "refers primarily to the conscious, rational aspects of oneself" (55). It is the part of oneself that one thinks of as being essentially "me." To define the I is to define the obvious. It is what one means when one says "I" or "me" or "my." It is the part that knows, makes decisions, thinks, solves problems, remembers, deals with the outside world. I think, I feel, I talk, I remember, I act, I walk, I run, I sing. Freud says the I "is turned toward the external world, it is the medium for the perceptions arising thence, and during its functioning the phenomenon of consciousness arises in it. It is the sense-organ of the entire apparatus; moreover it is receptive to excitations from outside but also those arising from the interior of the mind" (67). In other words, the I perceives and reacts to the external world. (The "external world" is simply that part of the world that one has to deal with directly, all that which is outside one's body—varying from the hospital room of a patient to the whole world if one is the secretary of state.) The I can learn from experience. The I relies on memory and uses language to express itself. (Note: one could simply say, "I use language"; or "I remember what happened yesterday." The I is the personality part of the psyche, so if one is writing about a person or a character, one could refer to the I of the person by the person's name. Instead of speaking of Mary's I, one could just say "Mary.")

The It (Id)

In German Freud uses the everyday word for "it" ("das Es") rather than the jargonistic id, and so shall we. Bettelheim says that a German child was referred to as "it" "before he learned to repress many of his sexual, aggressive, and otherwise asocial impulses, before he felt guilty or ashamed because of them, before he felt an obligation to resolve contradictions and bring logical order into his thoughts; in short, it reminds him [the German reader] of a time when his entire existence was dominated by the it" (57). The it is largely unconscious. Freud says that the it is "filled with energy reaching it from the instincts"; the it strives "to bring about the satisfaction of the instinctual needs subject to the observance of the pleasure principle" (65). The it seeks to gratify the senses, the demands of the body for pleasure or for release from tension. The it craves immediate gratification, and, what is impossible, total gratification.

The it is the infantile part of the psyche; it does not change in the passage of time; it remains always a baby, so to speak. Freud writes that there is nothing in the it "that corresponds to the idea of time ... Wishful impulses which have never passed beyond the id, but impressions, too, which have been sunk into the id by repression, are virtually immortal" (66). No matter how old or mature a person becomes, one's it is always infantile.

The it is selfish and asocial. The it wishes, demands, puts pressure on the I to satisfy its cravings, but the it cannot relate to the outer world. The it depends on the I to carry out its urges. The it has no concept of reality. In fact, the it does not think or use words (only the I does that.)

And the it is amoral or unmoral (but not immoral). Freud says the it "knows no judgments of value: no good and evil, no morality" (66). The it is dominated by the pleasure principle. (Morality belongs to the I as pressured by the above-I.)

The it, Freud says, "is the dark, inaccessible part of our personality." The it is "a chaos, a cauldron full of seething excitations ... The logical laws of thought do not apply in the it, and this is true above all of the law of contradiction. Contrary impulses exist side by side, without canceling each other out or diminishing each other" (65).

The it cannot be entirely repressed or repulsed; the it needs healthy outlets. The I must meet and regulate the it's demands.

Keep in mind that the it belongs to a person's unconscious. It does not speak or think. The it wants, demands, needs, feels. The it puts pressure on the I—the person—to respond to the it's demands. The it is basically part of the unconscious. Do not think of the it as a separate personality.

The Above-I (Super-ego)

The term Freud uses for this part of the psyche is "uber-Ich," which can be translated as "above-I" or "over-I" or "upper-I." Bettelheim explains that the term "denotes an integral part of the person—a controlling and often over controlling institution of the mind which is created by the person himself out of inner needs and external pressures that have been internalized" (58). The above-I is similar but not quite the same as "conscience." Freud calls it "the observing agency," that part which watches over and approves and disapproves of the actions of the I.

The above-I is the result of the child's assimilation of his parents' standards of what is good and socially acceptable and thus to be striven for and what is bad and socially unacceptable and thus to be avoided. One of the first words any child learns is "no." Children learn from their parents, teachers, and other members of society that certain forms of behavior are not acceptable. Sometimes they learn through punishment or the threat (real or implied) of the withdrawal of the parents' love. Children learn to adjust themselves to the demands of their parents and of their social environment.

Freud says that in educating children (and by "educating" he means everything people convey to children by their words and overall behavior), people "follow the precepts of their own super-egos." Thus, a child's above-I "is in fact constructed on the model not of its parents but of its parents' super-ego: the contents which fill it are the same and it becomes the vehicle of tradition and of all the time-restraining judgements of value which have propagated themselves in this manner from generation to generation" (60). Thus children absorb the standards of behavior and expectations of conduct from the society in which they grow up.

As children develop, the external restraints put on them by their parents and others, Freud says, are internalized and the above-I "takes the place of the parental agency and observes, directs, and threatens the ego in exactly the same way as earlier the parents did with the child" (55). We begin with our parents saying "no" and "do that!" and we end by telling ourselves "no" and "do that!"

Freud further states that the above-I is the means by which the I "measures itself, which it emulates, and whose demand for ever greater perfection it strives to fulfill" (58). The above-I is "the representative for us of every moral restriction, the advocate of striving toward perfection" (59). It also motivates us to strive for approval first of our parents and then of society and people in general.

The above-I is largely, though not entirely, unconscious. The I is aware of pressures from the above-I and often puts into words these pressures to conform or to strive for perfection. The I may think, "I ought to do my homework," or "I should study this weekend rather than getting drunk." But much of the force of the above-I may be unconscious.

The above-I punishes and rewards. When a person behaves properly—that is, according to the demands of the above-I, the person is rewarded by good feelings, pride, a sense of accomplishment. When one does not meet the demands of one's above-I, one may feel guilt or shame. One may be depressed without knowing why. One may feel inferior to others.

The above-I makes no distinctions between thought and action and may punish a person for "bad" thoughts as well as "bad" behavior. The above-I does not care about the needs of the it or the need to conform to the external world. It is the I that must do these things.

The above-I is not rational. It may push a person in more than one way at the same time. The above-I may make one feel guilty if one does an action and guilty if one doesn't do the same action. As Mark Twain's Huckleberry Finn says, "it don't make no difference whether you do right or wrong, a person's conscience ain't got no sense, and just goes for him anyway. If I had a yaller dog that didn't know no more than a person's conscience does I would poison him. It takes up more room than all the rest of a person's insides, and yet ain't no good, no how. Tom Sawyer he says the same."

Keep in mind that the above-I is largely unconscious. It does not think or speak. The above-I puts pressure on the I—the person—who has to respond to its demands. The above-I is not a separate personality but mostly a part of a person's unconscious.

How the I Deals with the It and the Above-I

The I, unlike the it and the above-I, has to deal with the external world. The healthy I works for balance. The I needs to understand and satisfy the demands of the it. If the I tries to block or repulse the demands of the it, the it may explode in some other outlet, or the person may become neurotic. If the I yields too much to the it, the person may become overly impulsive. The I needs to find socially acceptable ways of expressing the demands of the it. The I also needs to adjust the demands of the above-I to the external world. A person who has an overly-developed above-I may become a slave to conformity or may have a severe guilt complex. The I may be repulsing the energy of the it which might give the person a more satisfying, fulfilling life. The I needs to form its own standards and ideals and free itself to some extent from the demands of society that are built into the above-I. It may be possible for one to develop an independent conscience, an inner voice of right and wrong, that is not so dependent on conforming to the expectations of society.

Freud did not think it was an easy task for the poor I to find a good balance between the it and the above-I. In the following passage Freud shows how hard it is for the I to deal with the it, above-I, and the external world; he shows the anxieties that the I experiences as the I struggles to meet the demands placed upon it. I have given first a short quotation from the passage—then I have rewritten the passage with the ego (the I) speaking directly about its problems of adjustment. As we all have similar problems of adjustment, think of the speaker as your ego, your I speaking, you speaking.

First, the first part of the passage (translated from German) as Freud wrote it:

> We are warned by a proverb against serving two masters at the same time. The poor ego has things even worse: it serves three severe masters and does what it can to bring their claims and d mands into harmony with one another. (69)

Then, the passage rewritten with the I speaking for itself:

> We are warned by a proverb against serving two masters at the same time. I have things even worse: I serve three severe masters and I do what I can to bring their claims and demands into harmony with one another. These claims are always divergent and often seem incompatible. No wonder that I so often fail in my task. My three tyrannical masters are the external world, the above-I, and the it … I feel hemmed in on three sides, threatened by three kinds of danger, to which if I am hard pressed, I react by generating anxiety. Owing to my origin from the experiences of the perceptual system, I am earmarked for representing the demands of the external world, but I strive too to be a loyal servant of the it, to remain on good terms with it, to recommend myself to it as an object and to attract its libido [life energy] to myself. In my attempts to mediate between the it and reality, I am often obliged to cloak the unconscious commands of the it with its own preconscious rationalizations, to conceal the it's conflicts with reality, to profess, with diplomatic disingenuousness, to be taking notice of reality even when the it has remained rigid and unyielding. On the other hand I am observed at every step I take by the strict above-I which lays down definite standards for my conduct, without taking any account of my difficulties from the direction of the it and the external world, and which, if those standards are not obeyed, punishes me with tense feelings of inferiority and of guilt. Thus, driven by the it, confined by the above-I, repulsed by reality, I struggle to master my economic task of bringing about harmony among the forces and influences working in and upon me, and we can understand how it is that so often we cannot suppress a cry: "Life is not easy!" If I am obliged to admit my weakness, I break out in anxiety—realistic

anxiety regarding the external world, moral anxiety regarding the above-I, and neurotic anxiety regarding the strength of the passions in the it.

One of the tasks of psychoanalysis is to help the poor I in its struggle. The goal is to "strengthen the ego, to make it more independent of the super-ego, to widen its perceptions and enlarge its organization, so that it can appropriate fresh portions of the id" (71).

Freudian Chart of the Psyche

It (id)—pleasure principle, bodily desires and instincts.

- Puts pressure on the I to gratify the senses, the demands of the body for pleasure and for release of tension.
- Wants immediate and total gratification.
- Causes neurotic anxiety if its needs are not met or if they are repressed; feelings of frustration, confusion, lust.

Above-I (super-ego)—puts pressure on the I to live up to its standards for behavior and expectations of conduct (usually to conform to society's expectations of what is good and socially acceptable).

- May demand perfection—social and moral.
- Punishes and rewards the I: rewards the I with good feelings when the I meets its demands and punishes the I with bad feelings (guilt, shame, sense of inferiority, depression) when the I fails to meet its demands.
- Causes moral anxiety if the I does not live up to the demands of the above-I, such as worrying about whether one has done the right thing and worrying about what other people think.

I (ego)—knows, remembers, thinks, solves problems, etc. Deals with the outside world.

- Satisfies the demands of the it in socially acceptable ways or in socially unacceptable ways or tries to suppress the demands of the it or indulges the it so much that one becomes impulsive.
- Meets or fails to meet the demands of the above-I.
- Feels realistic anxiety about the external world, worrying about such things as losing one's job or failing a course.

FREUDIAN ANALYSIS OF TWO BLAKE POEMS

In the first-person narration of poems, it is easy to identify the narrator or speaker with the I. The I of the work relates thoughts, perceptions, and memories. One may be aware of the pressures of one's it and one's above-I. One way to approach a piece of literature is to ask whether a character's I (or one could simply say character) has reached a balance between his or her it or above-I. The climax of the story may be either the balance or failing to achieve balance.

"The Little Vagabond" from *Songs of Experience* by William Blake

Dear Mother, dear Mother, the Church is cold.
But the Ale-house is healthy and pleasant and warm;
Besides I can tell where I am used well.
Such usage in heaven will never do well.

But if at the church they would give us some ale,
And a pleasant fire, our souls to regale:
We'd sing and we'd pray all the live-long day:
Nor ever once wish from the Church to stray.

Then the parson might preach and drink and sing
And we'd be as happy as birds in the spring
And modest dame Lurch, who is always at church,
Would not have bandy children nor fasting nor birch.

And God like a father rejoicing to see,
His children as pleasant and happy as he:
Would have no more quarrel with the Devil or the Barrel
But kiss him and give him both drink and apparel.

The speaker of "The Little Vagabond" by William Blake has a conflict between the it's demands for pleasure and the above-I's pressure for conformity and perfection. The ale-house suggests the it wants to be "healthy and pleasant and warm." The boy is ready to satisfy the needs of the it—he imagines a church that is as nice as the ale-house with a "pleasant fire"—a place where people could sing and be happy. He will meet the demands of the above-I by praying and singing in the church, rather than going to the ale-house. He has a sensitive above-I that sees the hypocrisy of the cruel people at church: "such usage in heaven will never do well." He sees dame

Lurch as a lady with a distorted above-I who uses birch to beat her children. The whole poem suggests an integrated person who can healthily express the needs of the it and adjust his above-I to the external world. The boy's vision is one of regaling the soul while satisfying the needs of his body. The last stanza compares God to a "father rejoicing to see/ His children as Pleasant and happy as he." Here God is like the above-I rewarding one for proper behavior. "The Devil or barrel" is an expression of the it, and here the boy imagines God (the I or the above-I) meeting the demands of the it by giving it "both drink and apparel." All is harmony.

"I Saw a Chapel All of Gold" by William Blake

I saw a chapel all of gold
That none did dare to enter in;
And many, weeping stood without,
Weeping, mourning, worshipping.

I saw a serpent rise between
The white pillars of the door;
And he forced and forced and forced
Down the golden hinges tore.

And along the pavement street
Set with pearls and rubies bright
All his slimy length he drew
Till upon the altar white

Vomiting his poison out
On the bread and on the wine.
So I turned into a sty
And laid me down among the swine.

The last two lines of "I Saw a Chapel All of Gold" by William Blake clearly indicate that the speaker's I has not reached a healthy, integrated balance. The speaker seems to have a weak I with an it he cannot control and with a severely punishing above-I. Because he cannot live up to the standards and expectations of his above-I, his above-I punishes him by making him feel inferior and guilty: he is no better than a pig and might as well sleep in a sty. It may even be that his above-I has driven him to commit or think about committing some nasty action—present in his vision in symbolic terms—in order to punish him for his failure to meet the strict demands of the above-I. The above-I has led him to the ultimate punishment, self-destruction.

If we look at the poem in a slightly different way, we can see the speaker's vision as the it's reaction to the efforts of the I to suppress the it. The serpent with its "slimy length" suggests the it. Instead of accepting his it as an essential and vital part of his psyche, the speaker, overwhelmed by the pressures of the above-I, sees the it as evil and disgusting. At the same time his efforts to repulse the it have driven the it to an outburst, to a violent attack on the self.

The imagery of the poem is first of all religious. The gold chapel, the "white pillars," "the golden hinges," "pearls and rubies" (which seem to allude to the last chapter of the Book of Revelation), and the "altar white" suggest the holy, the precious, and the pure. The serpent breaks into the chapel, drags its "slimy length" over the pavement, and vomits its poison on the bread and wine, the most sacred symbols of the Christian church, the body and blood of Jesus. One can see all of this as the it's reactions to being repulsed. The it breaks out and forces itself on the I in an ugly and destructive way.

The imagery is also obviously sexual. The serpent with its "slimy length" is a **phallic symbol** (a term used for anything that resembles an erect penis). The serpent rapes the wombic chapel. He "forced and forced and forced/ down the golden hinges tore" is clearly a description of sexual assault. "Vomiting his poison out" is the ejaculation of semen. The sexual imagery indicates the disgust the speaker feels about his it. Perhaps his problem is that he cannot accept his sexual nature and drives, seeks to repress them only to discover that these urges will make themselves felt regardless of the censorship of the above-I.

Some of the above interpretation may appear to be somewhat inconsistent, but the poem plainly reveals an unbalanced individual, unable to accept the sexual and pleasure-seeking part of himself, his it, and tormented by the above-I. The poor I has been defeated by the it and the above-I and gives up in despair: "So I turned into a sty/ And laid me down among the swine."

FREUDIAN ANALYSIS OF CHARACTER—GUIDING QUESTIONS

The following may be applied to any character in a story (narrative poem, short story, novel, or play):

- Analyze whether the character is a balanced or unbalanced person. You might focus on the end of the work, especially a longer one; you might contrast the characters' states of mind at the beginning with their states of mind at the end.
- How effective is the character (the I) in dealing with the external world? Does the character find satisfactory outlets for the it? Or does the character express the it in negative and destructive ways? Does the character attempt to repress or suppress the it? Or does the character indulge the it, becoming overly impulsive?
- How are the effects of repressing the it or indulging the it revealed in the character's actions and state of mind?
- How does the character adjust the demands of the above-I to the external world? Is the character ruled and tormented by the above-I, feeling shame or guilt? Does the above-I reward the character for satisfying its demands? Does the above-I pull the character in more than one direction? Is the character, perhaps by the end of the work, able to absorb some of the above-I into his or her I, becoming less a slave to the above-I and becoming a stronger person who is able to adjust the demands of the above-I to the external world in his or her own individual way?
- Finally, how strong or weak is the I? Does the character have a stable or unstable identity?

THE OEDIPUS COMPLEX

The Story of Oedipus

To understand Freud's Oedipus complex, one needs to know the story of Oedipus. The best known version and the one that most influenced Freud is Sophocles' Oedipus Tyrannos. Before Oedipus is born, an oracle from the priest of Apollo announces that the son will kill his father Laius, the king of Thebes. When the child is born, the father pins his ankles together and leaves the child to die on a lonely mountain. The child is found by a shepherd, who gives him to the king and queen of Corinth, who bring him up as their own son, not telling him he has been adopted. When Oedipus is a young man, a drunk at a feast tells him that his so-called parents are not his real parents. Oedipus questions his parents who deny the story. Then he goes to an oracle of Apollo, who tells him that he will kill his father and marry his mother. Greatly shocked at this revelation, Oedipus leaves home so that he will not do these vile things. On his travels an old man in a chariot rudely tries to force Oedipus out of the way; he attacks Oedipus, who in anger kills the old man and his servants. The old man is, of course, Oedipus' father Laius. When Oedipus arrives in Thebes, he solves the riddle of the sphinx; and as a reward gets to marry the queen, a recent widow. The queen is his mother Jocasta. Oedipus and his mother live together happily for many years; they have two sons and two daughters. Oedipus rules well and is dearly loved by his people. When Sophocles' play begins, Oedipus is attempting to find the cause of the plague that is killing his people. Step by step, he discovers that he is the cause of the plague; he is the shameful man who has killed his father and married his mother. His mother hangs herself; Oedipus puts out his eyes and demands to be sent into exile.

Freud's Oedipus Complex

Freud felt that the myth reveals the ambivalent feelings a child has toward his parents. On an unconscious level the child both loves and hates them. The boy wants to possess his mother and desires to kill his father. The girl, like the boy, begins with a deep, even sexual attraction toward her mother, and later wants her father as a love object and resents her mother. The result of these repressed hostile and incestuous desires is guilt and anxiety. A child who does not resolve the Oedipus complex may have severe problems of adjustment in later life.

All children have a strong attachment to the mother. In his early years the boy loves his mother and identifies with his father. The boy develops the Oedipus complex at about five when he reaches the genital period. At that time the boy's desire for his mother increases as does his hostility toward his father. He sees his father as a rival and wishes to be free of him so that he can take his father's place with his mother. However, he begins to fear that his father in retaliation may castrate him. Freud says that the threat of castration compels the child to abandon his desire for his mother and his hostility toward his father, and the result is that under the fear of "losing his penis, the Oedipus complex is abandoned, repressed, and, in the most normal cases, entirely destroyed, and a severe super-ego is set up as its heir" (114). In the "most normal cases" the boy is able to maintain an affectionate relationship with his mother and is again able to identify himself with his father.

The object of the girl's love is at first her mother. But as the girl gets older, she turns away from her mother and develops a strong attachment to her father. The girl's hostility toward her mother is partly the result of her mother's withdrawal of breastfeeding and of her jealousy of the mother's love for her other children or the mother's giving her attention to others.

(The same could be said for boys.) When girls discover that they do not have a penis, they may feel they have been castrated and may "fall victim to 'envy for the penis', which will leave ineradicable traces on their development and the formation of their character ... (110)." (This is the origin of the penis-envy concept.) She blames her mother for her "castration" and turns to her father, hoping he will give her the penis that her mother has denied her. Her Oedipus complex is not so easily resolved as the boys, but it becomes weaker with time, and the girl is able to recover much of her identification with her mother and have an affectionate relationship with her father.

How much of the above is true is debated by psychologists and others. Many feminists in particular think that Freud had an inadequate understanding of women and reject his account of the girl's penis envy. But most would agree that children do have ambivalent, even sexual feelings, toward their parents and that these attitudes toward parents change as the children mature.

LIFE AND DEATH DRIVES

Freud thought that much of the tension in the psyche comes from the conflict of the life and death drives. (Usually *Trieb* is translated as "instinct" in English, but even the footnote in *The Standard Edition* states the word in German means "drive.") Bettelheim defines the death drive as a "mostly unconscious drive or impulse that provokes us to aggressive, destructive, and self-destructive actions" (107). It is opposed by the life drive, which Freud calls "Eros." The life drive, the Eros, as Freud states, consists of the "erotic instincts [drives], which seek to combine more and more living substance into even greater unities," while the death drive opposes "this effect and lead[s] what is living back into an organic state" (95).

Bettelheim sees the struggle between the life and death drives as giving meaning and richness to life:

> Freud's system in its later development establishes the concept of an eternal struggle between the life and death drives in us and recognizes the need to help the life drive prevent the death drive from damaging us. It is this struggle which makes emotional richness possible; which explains the multifarious nature of a man's life; which makes alike for depression and elation; which gives life its deepest meaning. (109)

Works Cited

Bettelheim, Bruno. *Freud and Man's Soul.* New York: Vintage, 1984.

Freud, Sigmund. *New Introductory Lectures on Psychoanalysis.* Trans. James Strachey. New York: Norton, 1965.

6

ARCHETYPAL APPROACH TO LITERATURE

COLLECTIVE UNCONSCIOUS AND ARCHETYPES

Carl Jung (1875-1961), a Swiss psychologist who was influenced by Freud in his early career, later formed his own system of psychology. Jung emphasized the collective unconscious and archetypes. In *The Archetypes and the Collective Unconscious* Jung says that each person is born with a collective unconscious, which is not individual but universal: "it has contents and modes of behavior that are more or less the same everywhere, and in all individuals." Unlike one's personal unconscious, which is unique for each person and which is created out of one's own experience, we all share a collective unconscious. The contents of the collective unconscious consist of archetypes, which Jung defines as "archaic" or "primordial types," "universal images that have existed since the remotest times." The archetypes are universal symbols. He further says, "The archetype is essentially an unconscious content that is altered by becoming conscious and by being perceived, and it takes its color from the individual in which it happens to appear" (3-5).

In *The Forgotten Language*, Erich Fromm explains archetypes as resulting not from biological inheritance but from the common experiences of human beings. A universal symbol "is rooted in the experience of the affinity between an emotion or thought, on one hand, and a sensory experience on the other... The universal symbol is rooted in the properties of our body, our senses, and our mind, which are common to all men ..." Because we are similar physically and emotionally and because simply living on the planet Earth gives us certain similar experiences, we share "the language of the universal symbol" (15-16).

Archetypal Images, Persons, and Patterns

Following are descriptions of some major archetypes. A chief source for these descriptions is *A Dictionary of Symbols* by J.E. Cirlot. Another source quoted occasionally is *A Dictionary of Symbols* by Tom Chetwynd.

Cirlot emphasizes that archetypes frequently come in pairs so that one archetype is the opposite of another—for example, male/female; summer/winter; day/night. The relationship between contrasting archetypes can take three forms: tension between opposites, ambivalence (two aspects at once), and unity or synthesis. Also, an archetype can have either negative or positive connotations, depending on its context.

Keep in mind that in examining a piece of literature, one must examine each image individually and in context of the work. Not all images have archetypal significance. Do not distort the work by reading into it an archetypal meaning that does not fit the work.

CENTER ARCHETYPE/THE SPIRITUAL REALM/ THE REALM OF ETERNITY—"To leave the circumference for the centre is equivalent to moving from the exterior to the interior, from form to contemplation, from multiplicity to unity, from space to spacelessness, from time to timelessness" (Cirlot 40). The realm of the spirit that transcends time and space. Mystical reality. Eternity. The realm of the true self, the realm of God. Primary symbol: the circle.

COLORS—Chetwynd: "Whatever you spontaneously associate with a particular color will usually be an indication of its symbolic significance." Not all uses of color are archetypal. The intensity of the color may change its archetypal significance. Many color differences may be cultural rather than archetypal.

- RED (color of blood and fire). Intensity of life. Sexual passion. Love. Pain and injury. Anger.
- BLUE (the color of the sky). Reflection, truth, devotion, innocence, religious feeling, security. Coldness. Distance.
- GREEN (the color of living things, of grass, plants, leaves.) Life, fertility. Growth.
- Negative aspects: death, decay.
- YELLOW (the color of the sun). Illumination, intellect. Intuition.

DARKNESS AND LIGHT—Jung says, "Day and light are synonyms for consciousness, night and dark for the unconscious" (*Archetypes* 167).

DARKNESS (black)—associated with the night. The unknown, fear, death, nothingness, chaos, disorder. Evil, sin. Sorrow. Positive side: "Black, in fairly generalized terms, seems to represent the initial, germinal stage of all Processes" (Cirlot). A time of quiet or peace before birth or rebirth. The womb. Security, absence of conflict, peace. The passive.

LIGHT (white)—associated with day. Illumination, wisdom, understanding. Innocence, cleanliness, purity, salvation, happiness. Life. Order, reason. Warmth. The active. "Perhaps the most basic symbol of conscious life" (Chetwynd 242). Negative side: death, paleness, absence of life, coldness, frigidity. A blinding light can suggest the negative side of darkness.

DEATH/REBIRTH—The pattern of death followed by rebirth is perhaps suggested by the seeming death of the sun (thought to be a god in ancient mythology) and his return at dawn. This pattern is also suggested by the cycle of the year, as spring follows winter. The pattern can be seen in many stories where a character moves from a kind of death—incomplete or undeveloped life—to a new, more fulfilling life. The pattern provides the main structure for the archetypal journey of the hero (see below). The pattern is always being reversed; winter follows spring; night follows day; and inevitably old age and death follow youth.

DESERT—Absence of life, sterility, meaninglessness. But also the domain of the sun, thus virility, passion, immortality.

FALL INTO EXPERIENCE—A person falls from a state of innocence, simplicity, or ignorance and participates in the complexity of life. This fall is not necessarily a fall from good to evil. One may regret the loss of the state of innocence but know that one cannot return to it. One may accept the complexity of life as a challenge and the fall can be a kind of rebirth.

Another archetypal approach to the fall is seeing the fall as the result of a basic crime—such as eating the forbidden fruit in the story of Adam and Eve. Chetwynd says the basic crime is "becoming conscious, acquiring a rational mind." Thus, one loses one's "basic instinctive animal existence" (110). One loses one's childlike wholeness and spontaneity, becomes a conscious, rational creature, knowing, unlike animals, that one is going to die.

FATHER—According to Jung, "the father represents the world of moral commandments and prohibitions ... The father is the representative of the spirit, whose function it is to oppose pure instinctuality. That is his archetypal role ... hence he is very often an object of neurotic fears for the son" (*Symbols* 260-261). This concept of the authoritarian father is related to Freud's concept of the above-I or super-ego. A more positive image of the father might be a GOOD FATHER, a person who watches over his children with love and compassion. If there is a good father archetype, he might possess some of the qualities of the good mother.

FIRE—Energy, passion, power, warmth. A symbol of "transformation and regeneration" (Cirlot 105). Negative: destruction and terror.

GOOD FRIEND—The good friend is usually a member of the same sex who helps one to develop as an individual. The good friend, like the wise old man and woman, can be relied on in a crisis and can help one to use one's own resources. The good friend may be looked on as an alter ego—a person with a somewhat contrasting personality who completes or complements one's own personality.

INNOCENCE ARCHETYPE/ THE DREAM OF THE GOLDEN AGE/ THE GARDEN OF EDEN—A time or place where everything is provided. A paradise on earth. A place of innocence and safety. A place where one, like a child, is secure and protected by one's family or by God. The Golden Age, Cirlot says, "stands for life in unconsciousness, for unawareness of death and of all the problems of existence, for the 'Centre,' which precedes time, or which, within the limitations of existence, seems to bear the closest resemblance to paradise" (5).

OUTCAST or SCAPEGOAT—The scapegoat was an animal on which was placed the sins of the community. The animal was then driven out of the community, taking the sins of the community with it. A human scapegoat is one who is driven from the community to purify it of sin. Scapegoats become wanderers from place to place and may die on their journey for the sins of the people.

STRANGER—The stranger comes from the outside, usually from an unknown place, perhaps a superior place. The stranger may even be a god in disguise. The stranger brings the possibility of change. The stranger may upset the status quo and thus be seen as a threat to the community. But the stranger may bring the possibility of renewal, of a new start, of a new way of looking at and organizing things.

SUN—(related to FIRE) In northern countries, "... a warm life-giving, protecting loving power"; in southern countries "a dangerous and life threatening power from which man must protect himself" (Fromm 19). "The sun is the father-god from whom all living things draw life: he is the fructifier and creator, the source of energy for our world" (Jung *Symbols* 121). The active and masculine principle. Since the sun appears to die each night but always returns the next day, the sun symbolizes rebirth, immortality, protection, salvation. Sunrise: birth, beginning; sunset: death, ending.

TREE—Like any plant, the tree symbolizes life and growth. "In its most general sense, the symbolism of the tree denotes the life of the cosmos: its consistence, growth, proliferation, generative and regenerative processes. It stands for inexhaustible life, and is therefore equivalent to a symbol of immortality" (Cirlot 347). Jung on the tree: "Taken on average, the commonest associations to its meanings are growth, life, unfolding of form in a physical and spiritual sense, development, growth from below upwards and from above downwards, the maternal aspect (protection, shade, shelter, nourishing fruits, source of life, solidity, permanence, firm-rootedness, but also being 'rooted to the spot'), old age, personality, and finally death and rebirth" (*Alchemical* 272). Negative: leafless, seemingly dead.

TRICKSTER FIGURE—Tricksters love to play jokes on people; they like tricks and mischief for their own sake and are constantly getting in trouble with people and authority. They indulge their "its" (ids). They take advantage of other people's gullibility and like to make them look like fools. They frequently get away with all kinds of mischief, but eventually they go too far and suffer reversal, often at the hands of those they make their victims. Jung describes the trickster as "both subhuman and superhuman, a bestial and divine being, whose chief and most alarming characteristic is his unconsciousness. Because of it he is deserted by his (evidently human) companions, which seems to indicate that he has fallen below their level of consciousness" (*Arch* 263).

WATER—Positive: the source of life, of regeneration fertility. Purification, cleansing.

Negative: a source of death (storms, floods, drowning, stagnant water). Sometimes death followed by rebirth as in the story of Noah and the flood. Jung says that water is "the commonest symbol for the unconscious" (*Arch* 18). And since life comes from water, water also has a maternal aspect associated with the unconscious (*Symbols* 218-219).

WISE OLD MAN or WISE OLD WOMAN—"The old man always appears when the hero is in a hopeless and desperate situation from which only profound reflection or a lucky idea ... can extricate him. But since, for internal and external reasons, the hero cannot accomplish this himself, the knowledge needed to compensate the deficiency comes in the form of a personified thought, i.e., in the shape of a sagacious and helpful old man" (Jung *Arch* 217-218.) Thus, by relying on the wise old man, heroes learn to develop and trust their own inner resources. The wise old man is an external form of the hero's own potential. The wise old woman (not found in

Jung) may in the same way help the female hero to develop her abilities and self-reliance. She may be another form of the good mother.

Or perhaps, one should just call this archetype the wise old person, since what matters is not the gender of the helper but the age and experience and wisdom of the older person who helps younger persons to learn to trust themselves.

WOMAN—(In works of literature, a character may see a woman as being one of these archetypes; or a woman may see herself as one of the archetypes; or the narrator may present the character as an archetype.)

GOOD MOTHER—Fertility, fruitfulness, nourishment; protection, sympathy, devotion, awe, the intuitive. According to Jung, the qualities associated with the mother archetype are "maternal solicitude and sympathy; the magic authority of the female; the wisdom and spiritual exaltation that transcend reason; any helpful instinct or impulse; all that is benign, all that cherishes and sustains, that fosters growth and fertility" (*Arch* 82). Also, he says that the woman archetype stands for the "goal of our longing for redemption" (*Arch* 81).

BAD MOTHER—"On the negative side the mother archetype may connote anything secret, hidden, dark: the abyss, the world of the dead, anything that devours, seduces, and poisons, that is terrifying and inescapable like fate" (*Arch* 82).

TEMPTRESS—(a version of the bad mother) Lures persons away from their true selves. The negative aspect of the unconscious.

SOUL MATE OR ANIMA—another aspect of the Good Mother. The true self sometimes personified in a woman who helps the hero to find himself. (More on anima below).

Archetypal Analysis of Blake's "A Poison Tree"

"A Poison Tree" from *Songs of Experience* by William Blake

I was angry with my friend:
I told my wrath, my wrath did end.
    I was angry with my foe: I told it not,
    my wrath did grow.
    And I watered it in fears.

Night & morning with my tears;
And I sunned it with smiles,
And with soft, deceitful wiles.

And it grew both day and night,
Till it bore an apple bright;
And my foe beheld it shine,
And he knew that it was mine.

And into my garden stole
When the night had veiled the pole:
In the morning glad I see
My foe outstretched beneath the tree.

The Speaker of William Blake's "A Poison Tree" is a person who was not in touch with the archetypes but who now understands how he has betrayed his true self.

Angry with his good friend, he tells the good friend of his anger, and perhaps through his friend's help, he overcomes his anger. But angry with his "foe," he is unable to express his anger, which grows in his heart. Possibly, the "foe" represents a dark side of his self which he is unable to accept or express. His growing and repressed wrath becomes a metaphorical tree, which he waters and suns, until it bears a bright apple. On the surface the tree seems to match Jung's description of the archetypal tree—growth, life, nourishing fruits. The speaker waters the tree (water, needed for life) and suns the tree (sun, like water needed for growth). But the speaker has transformed the good tree into a weapon of evil. He distorts the archetypal and natural by using the tree for his revenge. The water is tears; the sun is the expression of his deceit as he fools the foe into accepting the tree as good. In the poem one pictures the tree as green and flourishing, matching the positive aspects of the archetypal tree. But in the picture that Blake used to accompany the poem, the tree is leafless, brown, dead and the foe is trapped under a fallen branch.

The speaker becomes a trickster in his tempting of his foe, leading the foe to envy and to covet what was "mine" and to break into the garden to steal the apple. The speaker succeeds in arousing greed in his foe and causes him to lose his true self.

The archetypal tree resembles the tree of knowledge of good and evil in the Garden of Eden. The garden that the speaker has created with its apple tree is an antithesis or parody of the dream of the golden age or the Garden of Eden archetype. Here innocence is only on the surface and the garden is a trap, a place which entices the foe to commit evil, to steal the apple. The apple, says Cirlot, "signifies totality; it is symbolic of earthly desires, or of indulgence in such desires" (14). The foe who seeks totality finds such indulgence fatal—the apple is poisoned.

The crime of stealing the apple which leads to the crime of killing the foe takes place at night, in darkness, signifying fear, death, and evil.

The main archetypal pattern in the poem is the fall into experience. The speaker in indulging his anger, his envy, and the dark side of his nature falls into an understanding of the complexity of life. The last lines indicate that he understands what he has done to himself: "In the morning glad I see/ My foe outstretched beneath the tree." The most shocking word in the poem is "glad"—glad to have committed a murder. But perhaps the speaker understands now how he has violated his own soul by his action, and he understands now that repression of one's emotions may lead to unnatural distortions and indulgences. And maybe he has even reached in this understanding a kind of rebirth in that he knows where and how he failed and has learned from his experience—the death/rebirth pattern.

THE ARCHETYPAL HERO AND HIS JOURNEY

The following is Joseph Campbell's summary of the archetypal hero from his book *Hero With a Thousand Faces*. Campbell acknowledges his debts to both Freud and Jung in formulating his ideas on the hero.

> The mythological hero, setting forth from his commonday hut or castle, is lured, carried away, or else voluntarily proceeds, to the threshold of adventure. There he encounters a shadow presence that guards the passage. The hero may defeat or conciliate this power and go alive into the kingdom of the dark (brother-battle, dragon-battle; offering, charm), or be slain by the opponent and descend in death (dismemberment, crucifixion). Beyond the threshold, then, the hero journeys through a world of familiar yet strangely intimate forces, some of which severely threaten him (tests), some of which give magical aid (helpers). When he arrives at the nadir of the mythological round, he undergoes a supreme ordeal and gains his reward. The triumph may be represented as the hero's sexual union with the goddess-mother of the world (sacred marriage), his recognition by the father-creator (father atonement), his own divinization (apotheosis), or again—if the powers

have remained unfriendly to him—his theft of the boon he came to gain (bride-theft, fire-theft); intrinsically it is an expansion of consciousness and therewith of being (illumination, transfiguration, freedom). The final work is that of the return. If the powers have blessed the hero, he now sets forth under their protection (emissary); if not, he flees and is pursued (transformation flight, obstacle flight). At the return threshold the transcendental powers must remain behind: the hero re-emerges from the kingdom of dread (return, resurrection). The boon that he brings restores the world (elixir). (245-246)

In adapting Campbell's pattern, I have de-emphasized the mythological and tried to emphasize the universal characteristics of the hero. It seems to me that the following pattern works just as well for modern heroes or characters as it does for heroes in myths. It is a pattern that can be applied to both men and women. (The hero represents or could be everyone.) It is a pattern that can be usefully applied to many stories. Although the pattern is most often found in stories of young people undergoing the process of initiation, the pattern is also found in older persons who are reaching for higher levels of maturity or who are undergoing an identity crisis. The pattern follows Campbell's three stages: separation, transformation, and return.

Separation

The hero receives **a call** to go on a journey to another realm. The call is essentially to discover and develop the true self—to overcome one's weaknesses, to develop one's inner strengths, to become an integrated, whole person—a good person. The call comes from within, from the true self, although in some stories the call comes in outward form from the gods or from God. The call is constantly being heard, whether or not the hero is consciously aware of it or responds to it.

The call usually takes the form of a **quest.** The hero has difficult tasks to perform, the doing of which aids one in discovering and developing one's whole self.

The hero's journey to achieve the quest may take one to faraway and distant lands, but the journey is essentially an inner journey, one in which the hero moves toward becoming an integrated, complete person. It is an archetypal journey toward rebirth. The goal of the journey is to find the self.

A person may refuse the call. If one rejects the call, one's life begins to fall apart. Instead of reaching integration of self, one becomes disintegrated, confused, and unhappy. One is not able to find oneself.

The hero may have difficulty in understanding or even listening to the call. Because one does not clearly understand the call, one cannot respond to it, and one's life becomes a mess. As the call is basically to become a good person, one can misinterpret the call if one seeks primarily for material success. The disintegration and chaos that one's life falls into are signs that one has misunderstood the call. But if one persists in trying to understand the call and to commit oneself to it, one will work oneself out of chaos and be able to start on the journey. This stage of resisting the call may be a profound learning process.

Sometimes a **tempter** or devil figure will try to lead the person away from self-discovery and self-development to evil, the materialistic world, and ultimately self-destruction. Although the temptation comes from an outside person, in another sense all temptations come from within—one's own inner insecurities, lack of faith in oneself, fears and anxieties. If one succumbs to this temptation, one has archetypally "sold one's soul to the devil." "What shall it profit a man if he gain the whole world and lose his own soul?" are Jesus' words describing the individual who fails to heed the call. One might consider the temptation to refuse the call a kind of negative call, a call to surrender to the negative side of the self, **the shadow** (see below.) One who does not accept the call to become a good person and gives in to the negative part of the self cannot, of course, become a hero. The hero may however become a tragic protagonist like Macbeth or Othello.

The hero's first test may be understanding the call and accepting it. Resisting the temptation to distort or to refuse the call gives one the first strength one needs to start the journey.

The hero now accepts the call, crosses the threshold, and starts on the journey. Crossing the threshold is the stage of separation from the hero's world (thus from the old undeveloped self), the first step toward rebirth.

Transformation

On the journey the hero undergoes transformation. The hero develops by various trials and ordeals. Passing these tests helps one in building one's identity. The hero passes these tests by cultivating and practicing such virtues as courage, endurance, cunning or use of one's intellect, consideration of others, and trust and reliance on the gods or God or basically trust in one's own true self. The transformation is a learning process.

Sometimes the hero has to fight monsters or deadly foes. These creatures can be interpreted as arising from the dark side of the self. The hero is fighting monsters on the outside, but one is really fighting one's own inner weaknesses. "The hero's main feat," says Jung, "is to overcome the monster of darkness; it is the long-hoped-for and expected triumph of consciousness over the unconscious" (*Arch* 167).

What happens if the hero fails the tests? One may learn from one's mistakes and as a result grow stronger so that one will pass the test if given a second opportunity. However, the structure of this type of story usually creates expectations of victory; the hero almost always passes the minor ordeals, thereby gaining strength for the major ordeal. Perhaps the hero's passing of the tests gives hope to the readers that they too can surmount their trials in life. (Perhaps the tragic protagonist is one who strives to pass the tests but who because of some weakness fails to achieve the complete goal—again the cause may be a failure to understand the call itself fully).

The hero may be helped in one's journey by a woman or a goddess, who may represent the intuitive side of one's nature. The hero may be helped by man or a male god, who may represent the logical or rational side of one's nature. The heroes may also be helped by the **Wise Old Man** or **the Wise Old Woman**, who guide them in learning of wisdom and reaching toward maturity and by **the Good Friend.** Sometimes animals, which represent the hero's intuition, aid the hero. "The hero finds all the forces of the unconscious at his side" (Campbell 72).

The hero will undergo a supreme ordeal, a final test, the passing of which will complete one's rebirth. The supreme ordeal may be an actual or symbolic visit to the underworld. The underworld is a symbolic form of the dark side of the self.

Return

After one has proved oneself by passing one's ordeals and developed one's true self, one returns to the real world where one will be expected to put into practice what one has learned on one's journey. Now as an integrated, mature, whole person, one will know oneself and be beneficial to others and to society. The hero, says Campbell, "brings back from his adventure the means for the regeneration of his society as a whole (38)." The return is not easy; the hero may find it difficult to be the leader or person that one desires to be. The hero may later have to undergo the process of transformation again.

QUESTIONS TO CONSIDER WHEN ANALYZING THE ARCHETYPAL HERO

These questions can be applied to almost any narrative, particularly one in which the hero undergoes any kind of quest, or develops or matures in any way, and moves toward a rebirth, a strengthening of her or his identity.

- What kind of call does the hero receive? What kind of quest is the hero given? Does the call come from within or from some outer source? (Again, the call is always to discover and develop the true self—to develop one's inner strengths, to become an integrated, whole, and good person.)
- Does the hero have difficulty understanding and accepting the call? If he or she refuses the call, how does his or her life fall apart?
- When does the hero accept the call? Is there some point in the story where the hero crosses the threshold?
- How does the hero pass the various ordeals and trials he or she meets, and in doing so, how does the hero cultivate such virtues as courage, endurance, cunning or the use of one's intellect, and trust and reliance in the spiritual realm (God, gods, one's inner self)? By fighting monsters, real or metamorphical, how does the hero overcome her or his own weaknesses?
- Is the hero helped in the journey by someone of the opposite sex, by a good friend, by an older and wiser person, or by an animal? How do these helpers enable the hero to rely on her or his own resources, intuition, and inner self?
- Is there some supreme ordeal that the hero undergoes that completes his or her testing and brings about rebirth?
- When the hero returns to the real world, how does the hero put into practice what she or he has learned on the journey? How does the hero, now an integrated, balanced person, live a good life?

JUNG'S ARCHETYPES OF THE PSYCHE

THE SELF—Carl Jung defines the self as the totality of the psyche, the conscious and the unconscious. It is an inner guiding factor, a regulating center that leads the personality to maturity and wholeness and harmony and understanding. In *Ego and Archetype* Edward F. Edinger defines the self as the "ordering and unifying center of the total psyche (conscious and unconscious) just as the ego is the center of the conscious personality... The self is thus the supreme psychic authority and subordinates the ego to it" (3).

As a part of the archetype of the self Edinger sees other themes and images associated with it. (The source of these images is Jung's collected works.):

Such themes as wholeness, totality, the union of opposites, the central generative point, the world navel, the axis of the universe, the creative point where God and man meet, the point where transpersonal energies flow into personal life, eternity as opposed to the temporal flux, incorruptibility, the inorganic united paradoxically with the organic, protective structures capable of bringing order out of chaos, the transformation of energy, the elixir of life—all refer to the Self, the central source of life energy, the fountain of our being which is most simply described as God. (4)

The archetype of the self can be thought of as a guide to help a person reach greater wholeness of being.

THE EGO—the conscious part of the self. (Similar to Freud's ego or I.)

THE SHADOW—the hidden, repressed, and negative aspects of the personality. Our unconscious animal spirits and drives. The dark side, the irrational side of the self—potentially destructive. At the same time a source of strength, spontaneity, strong emotions, and deep instincts. Largely unconscious. (Similar to Freud's id or it).

In dreams Jung says that the shadow appears as the same sex as the dreamer. As Mary Ann Matoon says in *Jungian Psychology in Perspective*, one can become acquainted with one's shadow and bring it partially under conscious control. Or one can repress it and the shadow will express itself in "inexplicable moods, irritability, cruelty, and in physical symptoms" (26). One can project one's shadow or negative feelings on another person.

THE PERSONA—the conformity archetype. The masks we wear in society. What Jung refers to as "the outer face of the psyche." Our social personality. (Similar to the concept of the super-ego or above-I.)

Matoon defines the persona as "the part of the personality that one presents to the world to gain social approval or other advantages and to coincide with one's idea of how one should appear in public … it is the public face, determined by what one perceives to be acceptable to other people" (28). Jung says, "the persona is a compromise between individual and society as to what a man should appear to be. He takes a name, earns a title, represents an office, he is this or that. In a certain sense all this is real, yet in relation to the essential individuality of the person concerned, it is only a secondary reality, a compromise formation, in making which others often have a greater share than he" (Two Essays 158).

THE ANIMA AND THE ANIMUS—"The inner faces of the psyche." Jung believed that each person possesses qualities of the opposite sex. In order for one to be an integrated, well-adjusted person, one must express these qualities of the opposite sex in one's life. One begins by projecting the anima or animus on one's parent of the opposite sex and then later one projects it on others of the opposite sex who arouse one's feelings either positively or negatively.

THE ANIMA—M.L. von Franz in *Man and His Symbols* defines the anima as "the personification of all feminine psychological tendencies in a man's psyche" (186). Jung defines anima as "soul." "What is not-I," says Jung about the anima, "not masculine, is most probably feminine, and because the not-I is felt as not belonging to me and therefore is outside me, the anima-image is usually projected upon women" (*Arch* 27).

Positive: intuitive capacity for love, feeling for nature, a guide for the inner self, nourishing, wisdom (the aspects of the good mother). Negative: over-dependence, domination, seduction, loss of masculinity and independence. In Hermann Hesse's *Demian*, the narrator relates how a woman named Eva reflects his anima positively:

> My love for Frau Eva seemed to fill my whole life. But every day it manifested itself differently. Sometimes I felt certain that it was not she as a person whom I was attracted to and yearned for with all my being, but that she existed only as a metaphor of my inner self, a metaphor whose sole purpose was to lead me more deeply into myself. Things she said often sounded like replies from my subconscious to questions that tormented me. There were other moments when I sat beside her and burned with sensual desire and kissed objects she had touched. And little by little, sensual and spiritual love, reality and symbol began to overlap... Everything significant and full of fate for me adopted her form. She could transform herself into any of my thoughts and each of my thoughts could be transformed into her. (127)

If one is unable to assimilate the anima adequately into one's whole personality, the anima may take on negative aspects. One's life can become disordered and unbalanced.

ANIMUS—the personification of all masculine psychological tendencies in a woman's psyche. Positive: "initiative, courage, objectivity, and spiritual wisdom" (von Franz 206).

Negative: overemphasis on intellect and suppression of maternal and nurturing qualities, rigidity, drive for power, domination of other people. If one is unable to assimilate the animus adequately into her life, the animus may take on negative aspects. One's life can become disorderly and unbalanced.

Process Of Individuation

Jung defined individuation as the "process by which a person becomes a psychological 'in-dividual,' that is, a separate, indivisible unity or 'whole.'" The goal of individuation is knowing oneself as much as possible. The goal is expanding the ego to greater wholeness of self. To reach individuation one needs to learn to confront and accept the shadow and use its energies in socially acceptable and creative ways. One needs to (a) express one's anima or animus so that one can be a more integrated, complete human being; (b) express one's inner self in one's persona; (c) learn to know all aspects of one's self, both positive and negative. The goal is self-knowledge, self-realization, reaching wholeness of self. Some methods of approaching self-realization and wholeness are the study of one's dreams, religious experiences, and to some extent the process of the journey, trials and attempts toward the whole self.

THE JUNGIAN ARCHETYPAL TOPIC

The following is a list of questions to consider when analyzing characters' individuation. These questions can be applied both to characters who undergo a process of individuation in a story and to characters who fail to reach wholeness of self.

Has the character learned to confront and accept his or her shadow and use its energies in socially acceptable and creative ways? Or is the character dominated by his or her shadow, which the character has tried to repress or expresses negatively?

Does the character express the inner self in her or his persona? Or does the character's persona, her or his social roles, suppress the character's inner self so the character is somewhat artificial? (You might begin by analyzing the persona the character has adopted and then deciding how much the character's persona depends on his or her need to conform to what the person thinks society expects from him or her.)

Is the character able to incorporate the positive characteristics of the opposite sex (the anima or the animus) into her or his life? Or is the character distorted and unbalanced by repressing the characteristics of the opposite sex and trying to be too feminine or too masculine?

Does the character undergo the process of individuation, knowing himself or herself as much as possible, expanding the ego to greater wholeness of self?

SHE-HERO: A FEMINIST APPROACH TO ARCHETYPES

In her book *Archetypal Patterns in Women's Fiction* Annis Pratt shows that women, like men, receive calls to become integrated, whole persons but that the male-oriented or male-dominated cultures in which they must seek fulfillment frequently prevent their growth into true adulthood. In the following passage from her introduction she describes the sense of alienation she believes women feel in our western culture:

> ... [W]e are outcasts in the land ... we have neither a homeland of our own nor an ethnic place within society. Our quests for being are thwarted on every side by what we are told to be and to do, which is different from what men are told to be and to do: when we seek an identity based on human personhood rather than on gender, we stumble about in a landscape whose signposts indicate retreats from, rather than ways to, adulthood. In existential terms, our desire for responsible selfhood, for the achievement of authenticity through individual choice, comes up against the assumption that a woman aspiring to selfhood is by definition selfish, deviating from norms of subservience to the dominant gender. If authenticity depends upon totality of self—the greatest possible exercise of our capacities for significant work, intellectual growth, political action, creativity, emotional development, sexual expression, etc.—then women are supposed to be less than total selves. (6)

Her definition of "totality of self" in the last sentence is an excellent summary of what the hero is striving for in becoming a complete person. But women, Pratt suggests, while having the same needs and desires to be authentic persons, find it harder to achieve their goals in a male-dominated world that obstructs their journeys toward the true self.

Below are summaries of some of the archetypes she finds in women's fiction, but which I think also can be found in perceptive novels by men. Since she is writing exclusively of women characters, the word hero always refers to a female character. In order to make these archetypes more universal, I have sometimes added comments (in parentheses) to show how the archetypes might be applied to all persons, to both sexes.

Female Hero Archetypes

THE GREEN WORLD AND THE GREEN-WORLD LOVER—By the **green world** Pratt means nature, a safe place for the adolescent girl who has a difficult time adjusting to the demands of her society. The green world may take the form of an island, a garden, a woods, or any green place where the person feels free or whole. The older woman returns to nature or the memory of nature for renewal. Women find "solace, companionship, and independence in nature ... Nature, then, becomes an ally of the woman hero, keeping her in touch with her selfhood, a kind of talisman that enables her to make her way through the alienations of male society" (21).

(The green world perhaps suggests **the Innocence archetype**, a place of innocence that one can remember and draw on as a source in the struggle for maturity. The archetype suggests a place where one can get away from other people, especially the opposite sex, where one can get in touch with nature or the true self.)

The **green-world lover** is the image of an ideal lover, a lover from the green world, not from the social world of expectations of engagement and marriage. The green-world lover suggests the possibility of sexual love and fulfillment. The green-world lover, who may be "an actual figure or a revery one, an ideal, non-patriarchal lover, sometimes appears as an initiatory guide and often aids at difficult points in the quest" [of the hero toward rebirth] (140).

GROWING-UP GROTESQUE ARCHETYPE—The young woman, who hopes and longs to be a complete person, to find a role in society which will enable her to exercise her abilities and desires, will usually find her growth toward maturity stifled by the limitations society puts on women. Her attempts to "develop independence are met with limitation and immurement, training in menial and frustrating tasks, restrictions of the intellect (lest she perceive her status too clearly), and limitation of erotic activity" (29). Instead of growing up whole, developing virtues and strengths by passing the tests and ordeals of life, she frequently grows up "grotesque," becoming a kind of monster instead of a whole human being; or rather she is not allowed to grow up at all. All too often, "growing up female" may be "a choice between auxiliary or secondary personhood, sacrificial victimization, madness, and death" (36).

RAPE /TRAUMA ARCHETYPE—Women are not only denied erotic freedom, they are frequently victims of rape. "The event of 'rape,' in that it involves the violation of the self in its psychological and physical integrity, thus becomes central to the young woman's experience even if she is to be bedded down legally, within a marriage" (24-25). A man (lover, husband, even father) can force his will on the woman, destroying her own freedom and ability to act as she chooses, destroying her sense of being her own person. Rape, which can be sexual violation but also psychological violation of her sense of wholeness, disrupts the "freedom, solace, and protection" of nature, the Green World, and damages the individual, sometimes permanently.

ENCLOSURE ARCHETYPE—Although Pratt does not discuss this archetype separately, she uses the term **enclosure** frequently. In contrast to the "green world of authenticity," the hero usually must live in the house to which the woman is primarily confined, the place where she must fulfill her gender role. It is a place dominated by the father or husband or other male-authority figure who stifles the freedom of the hero. The patriarchy opposes women's desires for erotic freedom ("the right to make love when and with whom they wish") (24). Marriage itself may become a limiting enclosure. Women lose their freedom to come and go:

> "which involves the right to make decisions about one's own time work, and other activities;... early lovers are banished, to be replaced by a husband who resembles the gothic villain; erotic freedom is severely limited; intelligence becomes a curse, and, correspondingly, too much consciousness of one's situation leads to punishment or madness" (45).

Another form of enclosure is the madhouse, the mental institution, a place of "suffocation, breathlessness, of being stuffed down and dwarfed" (35). The enclosure is a prison where the hero cannot escape the restraints put upon her (at least, symbolically) and cannot reach true maturity. (A positive version of this archetype would be a nest, a secure home, a place of safety, shelter, and nourishment, a place where a person would feel she belonged and could exercise her gifts and talents without feeling repressed or constrained, perhaps a place which she controls rather than a place where she is controlled.)

WISE OLD WOMAN—The wise old woman is a person who refuses to abandon her ties with nature and who has achieved selfhood through a "creative solitude. "She's usually a woman who has not married and who lives by herself—she has come to understand and accept herself as a whole woman, transmuting the polar 'male' and 'female' attributes into a new androgynous consciousness" (131). She may be a social outcast or misfit since she is not part of a couple or a family, but she also may have a "sense of energy springing precisely from this ability to release oneself from relationships, to allow oneself authentic individuality" (131). To the younger woman these older wiser women are figures of "repose and energy, individuality and strength, figures illustrating the eventual goal of her own quest for selfhood" (132).

DEMETER-KORE (MOTHER-DAUGHTER) ARCHETYPE—The myth of Demeter and her daughter Persephone (Kore, the girl) Pratt says "is of particular importance to women, uniting the feminine generations" (170). The story begins when the god of the underworld seizes Persephone while she is playing with and enjoying the company of women in a meadow, and takes her down to his kingdom, and forces her to become his wife. Her mother, the earth goddess of grain, mourns for her daughter as she wanders over the earth. Disguised as an old woman, she lives with a family for a while and takes care of a young boy whom she tries to make immortal but stops when the frightened mother objects. Demeter, grief-stricken at the loss of her daughter, brings famine and suffering to the earth, preventing the crops from growing. Finally, after the intercession of Zeus, the head of the gods, Persephone is returned to her mother, although she must go back to the underworld for one-third of the year. Jung states that both archetypes exist in all women: "…every mother, contains her daughter in herself and every daughter her mother, and that every woman extends backwards into her mother and forwards into her daughter" (*Arch* 188). By adding the wise old woman archetype to Demeter's disguise, Pratt says that we have a triple goddess, who is "virgin, maternal figure, and old woman at the same time… The fully matured feminine personality comprehends all three elements and can bring any one of them into play at any time" (172).

Works Cited

Campbell, Joseph. *Hero With a Thousand Faces*. Cleveland: Meridian, 1956.
Chetwynd, Tom. *A Dictionary of Symbols*. London: Paladin, 1982.
Cirlot, J.E. *A Dictionary of Symbols*. Trans. Jack Sage. New York: Philosophical Library, 1971.
Edinger, Edward F. *Ego and Archetype*. New York: Penguin, 1973.
Fromm, Erich. *The Forgotten Language*. New York: Grove Press, 1957.
Hesse, Hermann. *Demian*. Trans. Michael Roloff and Michael Lebeck. New York:

Bantam, 1965.

Jung, C.G., and Marie Luise von Franz. Man and His Symbols. Dell Pub. Co., 1968.

Jung, C.G. *Alchemical Studies*. Trans. R.F.C. Hull. Princeton: Princeton University Press, 1967.

---. *The Archetypes and the Collective Unconscious*. Trans. R.F.C. Gull. 2nd ed. Princeton: Princeton University Press, 1968.

---. *Symbols of Transformation*. trans. R.F.C. Hull. 2nd ed. Princeton: Princeton University Press, 1967.

---. Two Essays on Analytical Psychology. Trans. R.F.C. Hull. 2nd ed. New York: Pantheon, 1966.

Matoon, Mary Ann. Jungian Psychology in Perspective. New York: The Free Press (Macmillan), 1981.

Pratt, Annis. Archetypal Patterns in Women's Fiction. Bloomington: Indiana University Press, 1981.

7

FEMINIST APPROACH TO LITERATURE

PATRIARCHY

Based on Greek, the term **patriarchy** means the rule of the father. The basic unit of patriarchy is the family, in which a male (father, husband, or other authority) rules or dominates the wife, any other female relative residing in the household, and the children. The patriarchy is the system in which males dominate all parts of society—the government, education, business, institutional religion, art, science—indeed every aspect of culture. It is males who essentially have the power in patriarchy. It is females who are controlled, oppressed, limited, and restricted by the males. This control includes power over women's bodies, including their reproductive systems.

Patriarchy And Women

Feminists usually begin by analyzing patriarchy and its effect on women. In *Beyond Power*, Marilyn French sums up the powers that one needs to be a complete person. One needs to be educated, to move around freely in the world, to be able to decide what one will do in one's life: "Most basic of all is the power over one's own body—the right to be free of physical abuse, to control one's sexuality, to marry when and whom one chooses, or not to marry: to control one's own reproduction, to have rights over one's own children, and to divorce at will" (125). And in patriarchy women have been restricted in these rights.

In *Of Woman Born*, Adrienne Rich defines patriarchy as "the power of the fathers: a familial-social, ideological, political system in which men—by force, direct pressure, or through ritual, tradition, law, and language, customs, etiquette, education, and the division of labor, determine what part women shall or shall not play, and in which the female is everywhere subsumed under the male" (33). This quotation not only defines patriarchy but suggests how all individuals, male and female, are acted on by all sorts of pressures to conform to the gender role one's culture expects one to assimilate. One's sex depends upon one's biology, one's anatomy; but one's gender or sex-role depends on what one's culture expects of males and females. Kate Millett in *Sexual Politics* defines "gender identity development" as "the sum total of the parents,' the peers,' and the culture's notions of what is appropriate to each gender by way of temperament, character, interests, status, worth, gesture, and expression" (31). One is socialized and conditioned from early childhood, perhaps even from the moment of birth, to live according to one's sex-role. One internalizes these pressures and expectations of sex role so that one's basic identity depends on one's built-in concept of one's gender role.

In patriarchy, a woman's role is largely determined by her anatomy. She is expected first of all to be wife and mother. And she is also expected to raise the children and to maintain the home, to support the males in her family by caring for them, both physically and emotionally. As the old cliché goes, "a woman's place is in the home." In patriarchy, her status is almost always inferior to the male. If unmarried, she is expected to serve the family as daughter or perform some other domestic function. A woman is expected to be obedient to male authority; she is expected to suppress her own desires and needs of self-fulfillment in order that she might better serve the patriarchy. She is treated as a child rather than a socially responsible adult. She is usually expected to be chaste before marriage and sexually faithful to her husband and to devote herself to her family. She is even expected, as Rich says, to prepare the children to become part of the patriarchal system, to accept its values, and to "perpetuate it in their own adult lives" (36-37). Women are generally limited to the private sphere, the domestic realm, while the public sphere is reserved primarily for men. Millett says, "Sex role assigns domestic service and attendance upon infants to the female, the rest of human achievement, interest, and ambition to the male" (26). Women's work in the home is often seen as "nonvolitional," not of one's own choosing. They do work that "nature" requires of them. Their domestic work is basically not considered "work" (since it doesn't bring in money or material goods) and is unvalued. If women work outside the home, their jobs are usually extensions of the domestic realm (such as teachers, caretakers of the young) or work supporting the work of men. And women with outside jobs usually are responsible for the domestic work in the home.

Simone de Beauvoir in *The Second Sex* uses the term "the other" to describe how men think about women in patriarchy. A male thinks of himself as being "the absolute human type, the masculine." The male is "the Subject," "the Absolute," the essential human being. The female is "the other"—she is defined only in reference to man. He sees her basically as a sexual being: "For him she is sex—absolute sex, no less." She is "the incidental, the inessential as opposed to the essential" (xix). In other words, a woman is not quite human, not quite an individual, but a kind of alien other on whom man projects his needs and desires and also "all his moral values, from good to evil, and their opposite..." (223).

Adrienne Rich analyzes how patriarchal mythology has polarized women into two conflicting types. First, she is flesh, the sex, "the female body is impure, corrupt, the site of discharges, bleedings, dangerous to masculinity, a source of moral and physical contamination." She is also the mother, "beneficent, sacred, pure, asexual, nourishing ... " (13). She is good or evil, angel or monster. And women internalize these masculine ideas of themselves. They often see themselves in the same extreme ways men see them.

Women are stereotyped in many other ways. They are frequently associated with nature, while men are associated with control and reason. Thus women are irrational, impulsive, overly emotional, intuitive rather than intelligent, inconsistent, unstable, passive rather than active. The effect of stereotyping is that one does not see people as individuals. And it is easier to control people who are seen as types rather than as individual persons.

Perhaps, the most negative effect of patriarchy on a woman is its denial of her individuality, its repression of her need to be a fully developed person. Essentially cut off from any real power in the economic, political, and social system and limited to the domestic role of housekeeper and bearer and raiser of children, thought of as the "other," and stereotyped in various ways, she is frustrated in her longing for self-fulfillment. She may develop a negative self-image, interiorizing the negative way patriarchy defines and limits her. And, as Rich states, "powerlessness can lead to lassitude, self-negation, guilt, and depression ..." (40). In order to survive in patriarchy, Beauvoir suggests that women learn to dissemble their "objective actuality." They learn "from adolescence to lie to men, to scheme, to be wily ... " (292). They learn to hide their inner selves and real feelings from men. They develop shrewdness and other skills in order to survive in a male-dominated society, suggests Rich.

Of course, many of the above generalizations need to be qualified. Many women surely are successful in business, politics, and other areas. Many find self-fulfillment in the domestic realm, and many are perhaps happy in combining careers with family responsibilities. And one would like to think that our culture is changing so that women are gaining a more equal place in society. But on the whole I think we must recognize that our society limits and restricts women in many ways.

Men In Patriarchy

Marilyn French says that in patriarchy, all male structures of power are hierarchies. A hierarchy is "a series of ascending steps, a ladder or pyramid maintained by coercion and incarnating power and authority" (299). At the bottom are women; at the top are some superior men. Most men in a hierarchy are subject to men with greater power than they themselves have. The primary method that a hierarchy uses to maintain itself and to control the people within it is "the inculcation of fear" (303). Thus, in patriarchy men too are restricted in their freedom to be complete individuals since most men find themselves in a hierarchy with someone over them. (One might, however, point out that most men have women, either in public or private life, over whom they have some power.) Men too are restricted by the sex role patriarchy assigns to them.

What sex role is assigned to men? What does it mean to be a "man" in patriarchy? If women are assigned to the domestic realm, the public sphere belongs to men. If women are responsible for maintaining the home and the children, men are responsible for the rest of society. A man is defined by his work, his achievements, his success. If women are identified with the body and with nature, men are identified with the mind and with control of nature. If women are stereotyped as emotional and impulsive, men are stereotyped as rational and consistent. Men are defined largely by being what women are not.

In *The Male Experience* James A. Doyle analyzes the male sex role (particularly in American society) as consisting of four elements. The first element is the anti-feminine element. A little boy is taught very early not to "be like a girl." He is taught to avoid any behavior which might be identified as feminine. He is taught to avoid expressing any emotion that might be seen as showing weakness or vulnerability—emotions such as joy, love, compassion, tenderness, and fear (150). (He also learns that girls are not only different but bad and inferior.) He learns to avoid the more gentle emotions associated with women but is allowed to indulge in harsher emotions such as "anger, disgust, hostility, contempt, and cynicism" (155). A man must keep his fears hidden from other because fear is something women feel. Men must always appear to be brave and fearless. As a result of repressing their emotions, many men keep others "at an emotional arm's difference" (161). A man is motivated by his fear of being labeled "effeminate," called a "wimp" or worse "homosexual" and so must avoid doing anything considered "unmanly."

Marilyn French too feels that many men are repressed and lonely. Because they must appear to exercise control in every situation, because they are taught to suppress or repress emotion, and because they are expected to be extremely competitive, they are often isolated in a "solitary confinement of the emotions" (324). Many men remain adolescent. Many men overly rely on one woman, who offers sympathy, understanding, and support, for "all of their emotional nourishment," (325) but they are not equally supportive to that woman when she needs sympathy. They don't know how or can't listen to and respond to her when she wants support. Their relationships with their children may be restrained and stunted. They are not able to form close relationships with them; they are distant and absent.

The second element Doyle mentions is the success element. Males are pressured to win, to beat others, to be a success at everything. A boy should be good in competitive sports: a man should be a good breadwinner and rise to the top of his profession. If he fails at anything, he is unmanly. To achieve success, he must value competition, see others primarily as rivals, and work for the outward signs of success (e.g., high status or rank and material goods, like expensive cars and homes).

The third element is the aggressive element. He must be assertive and active, not passive like a woman. He must be ready to defend himself against others in a masculine way (183). He must avoid being called a coward.

Fourth is the sexual element. Men are expected to be interested, even obsessed, with sexual matters. A modern male is expected "to please and satisfy a woman's sexual needs" or be considered "no man at all" (138). Because many males put unrealistic sexual demands on themselves, they are unable to "learn to accept and enjoy their sexuality" (212).

Finally is the self-reliant element. A man is expected to be on his own, not relying on others. (Men don't like to ask for directions when they travel.) Under this heading "also fall toughness, courage, confidence, independence, determination, and coolness" (146).

A man may have a hard time living up to all the demands his sex role places upon him. He may fear ridicule from other males and even women if he appears to diverge too greatly from conventional maleness. He may leave undeveloped certain basic human traits and fail to be a complete human being. And how he sees himself and his role deeply affects how he sees and relates to the opposite sex—devaluing certain qualities in himself (that he thinks of as feminine) and overemphasizing other traits (masculine) leads him frequently to devalue women.

Finally, to see how a masculine code operates in patriarchy, we might examine how it works in the one of the first works of literature, Homer's *The Iliad*. The heroic code by which the hero lives is based on the hero's striving for honor and avoiding shame. First, the hero is simply a warrior, a fighter, a killer, a man. (A male who does not fight and kill is a coward, a non-man.) The honor of a hero depends primarily on his reputation as a fighter and the respect other men give to him. The greatest hero is the one who fights the most bravely, who kills the most men, and who has the most booty and prizes. He usually is skillful in words as well as deeds, speaking to persuade other heroes in council and bullying enemies with words in battle. Above all, the hero wishes to avoid shame which comes from failing to fight bravely (the most cowardly act being running from battle) and being dishonored by one's superiors. Behind the heroic code is the need to conform to society's expectations of manliness and the fear of being called cowardly, or worse, a woman. In this society men are highly competitive, not only against the enemy, but with each other.

The greatest hero in *The Iliad* is Achilles, who in the latter part of the epic kills men like a war-machine. But oddly enough, it is Achilles who is also the unhappiest. Dishonored by Agamemnon in the first book, he spends most of the epic brooding over his loss of honor. In the last book when the father of the man who has killed his best friend comes to him for the body of his son, Achilles shows some kindness and generosity that seems to go beyond the masculine honor code. He sympathizes with Priam, the old man, who reminds him of his own father. He shares food and wine with him, and promises that battle will stop for a few days so that Priam's son Hector can be honored. He even lifts the body of Hector onto a bier.

The Iliad serves as an example of how in patriarchy men are basically motivated by a code that forces them to conform to a rigid concept of manliness, but it also illustrates how a person, Achilles (even if only for a short time), can express qualities, such as compassion and sympathy, which are usually associated with women, and become a more complete, even a more human person.

FEMINISM

Feminism is a movement to win for women the same rights and freedoms that men have in patriarchy. In the 19th and early 20th century, women fought for the right to vote. Feminists, especially since the 1960s have been working for the end of discrimination against women in all areas of life and for equal opportunities in education, careers, politics. Annis Pratt writes that women want "totality of self—the greatest possible exercise of our capacities for significant work, intellectual growth, political action, creativity, emotional development, sexual expression ..." (6). "The personal is the political," one of the slogans of the feminist movement, means that the personal and political parts of life are interconnected, and women want to be free to make their own choices in both.

Ultimately, feminists seek to transform or destroy the patriarchal system and replace it with a system that emphasizes different, more humane values—values that are usually associated with the feminine. Marilyn French writes that feminists "*do not want women to assimilate to society as it presently exists but to change it*" (443). The opposite of a patriarchy is not a matriarchy, in which women rule and have power, but a system in which all people, regardless of sex, work together for the common good.

Feminists, of course, are not uniform in their beliefs or plans of action. And feminism is constantly changing in theory and practice.

Some feminists have emphasized the androgynous (from Greek—meaning male/female) approach. To free oneself from gender restrictions imposed by society, each person should, in addition to the basic qualities of one's own sex, develop the qualities associated largely with the other sex. In order to be a complete person, a woman should cultivate reason, initiative, courage, even aggressiveness, while a man should learn to be more compassionate and caring. (My own opinion is that we should stop labeling basic human traits as "masculine" and "feminine" and instead devote ourselves to the qualities that make a good human person, regardless of sex.)

Recent feminists have moved away from the androgynous approach and have stressed the values associated with women as superior and even necessary for saving civilization from destroying itself. Taken to an extreme, the masculine "heroic code," with its emphasis on male honor and competitiveness and domination of nature, could lead to nuclear destruction, or to utter pollution of the earth. Female values, such as sharing, cooperativeness, and caring for others, are, feminists believe, life-enhancing.

Associated with nature, the "feminine principle," French says, is "the pole of sexuality and bodily pleasure, of nutritiveness, compassion, sensitivity to others, mercy, supportiveness, and all giving qualities" (93). These are the positive aspects of the "feminine" that all human beings need to strive for. Instead of power, which is the motivating force behind patriarchy, we should devote ourselves to "pleasure." She defines pleasure as a joyful response to and participation in life. Pleasure is both physical and mental, derived both from using our senses and our minds. Pleasure can be found in many ways: in solitude and independence, in satisfying work, in being with others and sharing ourselves with them, in freedom in choosing our own way of life and in the responsibility of using our freedom constructively (538-542).

Other feminists also have asserted that women should emphasize "feminine" rather than "masculine" characteristics in their lives. Instead of being ruled by reason and logic, women should affirm the emotional, intuitive, even the nonrational sides of their nature. They should develop an integrative, flexible, holistic view of life. Instead of emphasizing individualism, women should stress interdependence of human beings upon one another—women should continue to develop their ability to relate to others. Instead of emphasizing competition, aggressiveness, authority and control, they should stress cooperation, working with others to settle differences peaceably, patience, and sensitivity to the needs and feelings of others—and perhaps, above all, nurturing and caring for others. (And one might add that these "feminine" characteristics are essential for all human beings, perhaps even for the survival of the planet.)

Finally, one of the goals of the feminist movement, particularly in America is, according to Cheri Register, "to create a feeling of sisterhood, a new sense of community among women, in order to overcome group self-hatred, the animosity that many women feel for others of their sex as a result of isolation, competition for male attention, and belief in female inferiority" (21).

Feminist Criticism—Analyze Patriarchy First

One basic approach of feminist criticism is the analysis of patriarchy in a literary work. How does the work of art reflect the values of patriarchy? Does the work criticize the effects of patriarchy on its characters, or does the work, perhaps unconsciously, support the basic premises of patriarchy? *The Iliad* as we saw in an earlier section, does make us question to some extent the masculine code which rules the lives of the heroes. Achilles, dishonored in the first book by the arbitrary action of Agamemnon, broods about the value of competition and the meaningfulness of awards and booty. He does goes back into battle near the end of the epic, winning great glory and honor, although he seems to behave like an inhuman killing machine. The epic, while probably confirming on the whole the masculine way of life, does show its extremes and limitations, and in Achilles' kindness to Priam at the end another side of life.

Complex works of art will usually be critical of the patriarchal system, at least in how it affects men. Feminists, though, think that most works by male writers are biased toward upholding the patriarchy, its structures and values. A feminist critic will attempt to expose that bias. In *Feminist Literary Studies: an Introduction*, K.K. Ruthven says that a feminist critic studies the ideology ("that never fully articulated system of assumptions by which a society operates," the purpose of which is to "justify the status quo") of male dominance in a literary work (31). The feminist critic examines "a literary work for traces of the ideologies which shape it, whether its author was aware of them or not," and points "to discrepancies between what the work purports to say and what a careful reading of it shows" (32).

Patriarchal bias may be reflected in conventional plots. An example is the quest plot, in which the hero proves his manhood by developing and exercising certain "masculine" virtues, such as courage and determination. The conventional ending of a comedy is a wedding, which suggests that a woman has found maturity by becoming a wife and a future mother.

Feminists are particularly interested in how a literary work portrays women. Does it show their oppression by patriarchy or does it support women's inferior status in patriarchy? For example, *The Iliad* shows that women are primarily treated as property. Briseis, the woman whom Agamemnon takes away from Achilles to make him understand his secondary place in the hierarchy, is primarily a prize, booty, whose removal dishonors Achilles. The narrator does not tell us how Briseis feels about being forced to go to Agamemnon's tent, supposedly for sexual service. Book 6, however, does dramatize for us the suffering patriarchy inflicts upon women. Andromache reminds her Trojan husband Hector how her father and seven brothers were all killed in battle—by Achilles—and how her whole life depends on Hector's survival in fighting. Both she and he know that when he loses the war, she and her son will become slaves of the Greeks. Andromache is presented essentially as the faithful wife of Hector, her identity and place in society dependent on his status. The epic, which mainly deals with the heroic world of men, ends, oddly enough, with the speeches of three women. Each woman states her pain, her personal loss. Andromache, for example, fears for her son, who will either be made a shameful slave or flung from the walls. She will be a slave. She regrets not having heard Hector's last words. However, while the narrator creates sympathy for these suffering women, the main effect of their speeches is to honor the great hero Hector, whose death they are lamenting.

Works by women writers will generally be more effective in showing women's oppression since, of course, women feel their oppression, while men at best can only understand it. Listen to Jane Eyre in Charlotte Bronte's novel voice her frustration with the male world:

> Women are supposed to be very calm generally: but women feel just as men feel: they need exercise for their faculties, and a field for their efforts as much as their brothers do; they suffer from too rigid a restraint, too absolute a stagnation, precisely as men would suffer; and it is narrow-minded in their more privileged fellow-creatures to say that they ought to confine themselves to making puddings and knitting stockings, to playing on the piano and embroidering bags. It is thoughtless to condemn them, or laugh at them, if they seek to do more or learn more than custom has pronounced necessary for their sex. (Ch. 12)

No man could have written those words. Jane Eyre shows how difficult it was for a woman in 19th century patriarchal England to make an independent life for herself. Outside of marriage, Jane Eyre knows that one of the few jobs open for a woman of her class is to be a governess, a position that was not only low-paid but frequently humiliating, since a governess was usually treated meanly. The above quotation shows how hard it was for a woman to find not only equality in a male-dominated society but also individual self-fulfillment.

One method of oppressing women in literature is to reduce them to stereotypes. Feminist critics examine how writers portray women, analyzing whether they are presented as complex individuals or type-characters. They particularly object to classifying women as either madonnas or whores, angels or monsters. If a woman is either a devil or an angel, and no woman or human being is perfectly good, then all women must be devils. They object to the archetypal depiction of them as good mothers, bad mothers, sirens and temptresses, and helpmates. These "archetypes" found primarily in male literature emphasize women only as they help or hurt men. As Gilbert and Gubar point out, reducing a woman to extreme archetypes "drastically conflicts with her own sense of her self—that is, of her subjectivity, her autonomy, her creativity" (48). A number of critics have suggested that archetypal women in male literature are usually projections of some part of the male's psyche rather than being individualized characters. Studying the role of women in male literature leads Showalter to conclude: "We are not learning what women have felt and experienced, but only what men have thought women should be" ("Poetics" 130).

Furthermore, some characterizations of women reveal an anti-female bias that needs to be uncovered and analyzed. According to Chris Weedon, feminist critics have shown how women in certain male fictions "are represented as passive, masochistic, and totally male-identified" (147). In these fictions, women exist primarily as sex objects for men, their function is to reveal or to bring out the male characters' masculinity. Female readers are encouraged to identify with these passive, sweet, weak, emotional heroines. Other fictions present women as strong, castrating, hostile, and destructive to men.

Since most literature written by men and even some literature written by women presents male experience of life as universal and female experience as secondary or supplementary to men, feminists stress that women should learn to read as women. Judith Fetterley analyzes the difficulties women have in reading novels in which readers are expected to identify with male heroes who are hostile toward women: "In such fictions the female reader is co-opted into participation in an experience from which she is explicitly excluded; she is asked to identify with a selfhood that defines itself in opposition to her; she is required to identify against herself" (xii). To read as a woman one must "become a resisting rather than an assenting reader, and, by this refusal to assent, to begin the process of exorcising the male mind that has been implanted in us" (xxii).

A related approach is to analyze the conventional gender roles of a society as revealed in a literary work and the characters' conflicts in adjusting to their gender roles and their attempts to get beyond gender restrictions to develop more complete personalities. For example, Jane Eyre longs to do something more with her life than making puddings, and Achilles stops killing for a while in order to be kind to an old man who reminds him of his own father (see above).

Feminists are mainly interested in women in literature, but what about stories in which there are no women? The absence of women may lead us to question the author's vision of life (a wholly "masculine" outlook that omits "feminine" values) or to fill in the gaps by finding the "feminine" values embedded in the text. Take, for example, the story of the prodigal son (Luke 15:1 1-32—see Chapter 3). There is a loving father welcoming his son. But where is the mother? Can not one imagine a heart-broken woman, silently yearning for her son's return? Suppose it was a prodigal daughter who was coming home, would the father be so happy to see a "fallen woman," more than likely a prostitute? (Perhaps, yes, considering that the teller is Jesus, who did show compassion to women of bad reputation.) If the forgiving father in the story suggests God the Father, some feminists might ask, "Where is God the Mother?" Another way of looking at the story would be to see that the father does exhibit certain "feminine" virtues, such as caring for others. The older son is more constricted by his masculine role, concerned chiefly about his status, his goods, and a narrow sense of justice which mainly means keeping all the property for himself.

Even if women are present in a text, feminists argue that male writers generally know very little about women's lives. Male readers and writers, as Annette Kolodny suggests in "Dancing Through the Minefield," have been ignorant of the contexts of women's lives (at least, in the past)—"the lying-in room, the parlor, the nursery, the kitchen, the laundry..." (155). Dale Spender in *The Writing or the Sex* says that even women have not been allowed to write about certain experiences in their own works: the joys, pains, and responses to childbirth, menstruation, and domestic work. Especially missing is the record of how women feel toward the men who have ruled their lives: "We know next to nothing about the attitude of ordinary women toward men who have commanded their conjugal rights—without regard to the health and happiness of their wives" (116). Novels may emphasize the everyday details of a man's life but seldom those of a woman's life. And one seldom finds in novels, particularly by men, quest stories in which a woman experiences self-discovery and self-development.

Feminists feel that they have been excluded from the literary establishment. The canon, the literary works that are included in anthologies and taught in literature courses, the "classics," includes very few by women authors. Men not only dominate the canon but also literary criticism. "Literary criticism," writes Dale Spender, "is an activity and a body of knowledge that is dominated by men; it was men who made up the rules, who constructed the theory and practice of 'lit crit,' who decreed what was good, bad, and indifferent long before they allowed women educational and occupational rights" (24). Feminists believe that male critics, although they pretend to be sexually neutral and assume that their techniques and criticism are universal, are really biased, and that this bias needs to be recognized and analyzed. Feminists, says Elaine Showalter, should move away from "male critical theory," which is "a concept of creativity, literary history, or literary interpretation based entirely on male experience and put forward as universal" ("Wilderness" 247).

The English language itself seems to exclude women. Words such as "man" and "mankind" suggest that women are not quite human beings. The use of the pronouns "he" and "him" to apply to both sexes in such constructions as "each person doing his best" (thanks to some 18th century grammarians) has the effect of leaving females out and suggesting that male experience is universal.

Feminist Analysis Of Patriarchy In Blake's "London"

"London" from *Songs of Experience* by William Blake

I wander through each chartered street,
Near where the chartered Thames does flow
And mark in every face I meet
Marks of weakness, marks of woe.

In every cry of every Man
In every Infant's cry of fear,
In every voice; in every ban.
The mind-forged manacles I hear

How the Chimney-sweeper's cry
Every blackning Church appalls.

And the hapless Soldier's sigh
Runs in blood down Palace walls.

But most through midnight streets I hear
How the youthful Harlot's curse
Blasts the new-born Infant's tear
And blights with plagues the Marriage hearse.

It is easy to read William Blake's "London" as an attack on patriarchy. Although the speaker is not identified as a woman and although our natural (or conditioned) inclination would be to think that since the writer is a man, the speaker, unless otherwise indicated, would be a man, I am going to refer to the speaker as "she." Although middle-class men in Blake's day would have more freedom to wander through the streets, especially at midnight, a sensitive woman, like a sensitive man, would probably have plenty of opportunities to observe the sufferings of the poor. The poem is constructed to make us share the compassion and anger at injustice that the speaker feels. And if we think of the speaker as a woman, even if that identification is somewhat arbitrary, we may feel even more sympathy for these victims of injustice.

The speaker wanders through the streets of London which the patriarchy has "chartered" (mapped, laid out according to a charter), even "chartered" the free-flowing river Thames. Everywhere the speaker turns in this "chartered" city, she "marks" the "marks" of weakness and woe in all the faces of the people she meets, people whom the patriarchy has oppressed, used, destroyed, and ignored.

She hears "the cry of every Man," which in 18th century language means every person. All the persons she hears are crying out from misery. The baby's cry is one of fear and she doesn't hear any motherly comforting. In every ban, which might refer to a wedding announcement or might mean a curse, she hears "mind-forged manacles"—signs of slavery, especially mental. It is not just one's body that suffers, but one's whole being, one's whole attitude to life, is in bondage.

In the third stanza the speaker attacks the state church and the state government, the main instruments of the patriarchy to control people. She marks how the cry of the chimney sweeper (a poor boy forced to go down filthy chimneys) "appalls" the churches he cleans. "Appalls" suggests that these churches are shamed, disgraced by their treatment of poor children. The churches, instead of being places of light and help to children, are "blackning," becoming black, evil by the dirtying of the chimney sweepers. The palace walls, suggesting the government headed by the king, are stained by the soldier's cry which "runs with blood." The cry of the chimney sweeper who does the dirty work of the church and the cry of the soldier who sheds his blood for the state are not heard by the patriarchy.

The speaker concludes her journey by emphasizing the suffering of women, illustrated by the curse of a young prostitute. Let's imagine the speaker as a middle-aged woman, almost certainly a mother, with some understanding of how society at that time forced young women abandoned by their seducers into prostitution or how poverty might make a family sell their daughter. She might understand how once a basically good girl or just a normal girl might have been corrupted by the life she has been compelled to lead. The speaker makes us hear "the youthful harlot's curse," the curse of a young girl who will not marry and will not bear legitimate children. Her curse is directed at the institution of marriage, which she as an outcast from the patriarchy cannot participate in. The marriage carriage to her is a "hearse," a carriage for the dead.

The speaker throughout the poem reveals how the patriarchy uses the poor for their own purposes—as chimney sweepers, soldiers, and prostitutes—and then abandons them. The patriarchy does not hear their cries. But our speaker hears and understands and makes us share her feminist values of "nutritiveness, compassion, sensitivity to others, mercy, supportiveness, and all giving qualities" (French 93). Even if we think of the speaker as a man, we can still feel compassion for these victims of the patriarchy.

Gynocritics (Women-centered Criticism)

Elaine Showalter in "Toward a Feminist Poetics," calls the first phase of feminist criticism "feminist critique": criticism concerned with "woman as reader" of primarily male literature, the literature of the patriarchy. The second type of feminist criticism she calls gynocritics" which is concerned with "woman as writer—woman as the producer of textual meaning, with the history, themes, genres, and structures of literature by women. Its subjects include the psychodynamics of female creativity; linguistics and the problem of a female language; the trajectory of the individual or collective female literary career; literary history; and, of course, studies of particular writers and works" (128). Gynocritics is an ambitious program, for it seeks not only to study female literature but also to find female ways of studying the literature.

One of the first projects of the feminist critics has been to rediscover female texts which have been ignored by the patriarchal literary establishment. After finding lost or neglected texts, critics reevaluate them from a woman's perspective and understanding. Partly, the feminists are seeking to expand the traditional canon with superior women writers, but even more they are working to find a meaningful body of literature that speaks to and for women. They have expanded the scope of what has been usually considered "literature" to include diaries, journals, letters, and other personal kinds of writing. They are also studying the oral culture of women—the stories, for example, that mothers tell their daughters. Non-white feminists, says Josephine Donovan, are especially interested in retaining "their racial and ethnic roots" and in preserving "authentic women traditions" and "the history and culture of their mothers" (159).

They are also writing new literary histories showing the influence of earlier women writers on more famous later women writers, partly to show the continuity of women's literary traditions. They study women's culture, past and present, for a better understanding of women's daily lives, to understand better the contexts, the settings of women's fictions.

Feminists are exploring new techniques for evaluating and analyzing women's literature. Some feminists are developing a more personal, intimate, even confessional, and more emotional style of writing that contrasts to the impersonal, rational style that conventional (male) tradition has favored. Women write differently from men, says Maggie Humm, because women think differently:

> ... [W]omen think in circles rather than lines, we tend to be holistic rather than partial; we prefer open to closed systems; we employ associational rather than sequential logic; we are obsessed with detail and pattern; that we write sentences to quote Virginia Woolf 'of a more elastic fibre than the old': that we are subjective and naturally attracted to interior spaces, children and animals. (14)

In writing criticism feminists want to break down the restrictions of institutional criticism for more experimental, more subjective reactions to literature. Feminists also use and adapt more traditional approaches. Kolodny suggests feminists should initiate "a playful pluralism, responsive to the possibilities of multiple critical schools and methods, but captive of none..." (161). Recent feminists have stressed the post-structuralist, particularly deconstructivist approach. (See Chapter 8.)

Feminist critics also encourage women writers to be independent in their art. Women should be free to relate their experiences completely, including details of everyday life, their mental and physical activities. They should explore the female realm, that private area of female life that is outside the male world. Register urges women "to forget literary convention when they create their female characters and to rely on their own subjective experience" (12). Register also suggests that women can create positive role models for women and present realistic solutions to female problems. Most important, a woman's literary work should be "authentic," giving a "realistic representation of 'female experience,' 'feminine consciousness,' or 'female reality'" (12).

The trend in feminism has shifted the emphasis from patriarchy's oppression of women to a celebration of women, their uniqueness, their values, their ways of looking at and understanding the world and themselves.

QUESTIONS TO CONSIDER IN FEMINIST LITERARY CRITICISM

- How does a literary work, directly or indirectly, show how patriarchy limits women, preventing them from becoming complete individuals?
- Does the work, consciously or unconsciously, support the basic premises of patriarchy, its structure and values? Does the work support women's ' inferior status patriarchy?
- How does a literary work, directly or indirectly, show how patriarchy limits men, limiting them as persons?
- How does the work indicate the sex or gender role expected by the characters' culture? Do the male characters in the work look on women as alien, as "the other"? Are the women characters presented as stereotypes rather than as complex individuals? Are the women characters limited to being angels or whores? Are the women irrational, impulsive, overly emotional, intuitive rather than intelligent, inconsistent, unstable, passive rather than active? How does the literary work indicate male stereotypes and the pressures the culture puts on men to conform to its expectations of masculinity?
- Is there an anti-woman bias in the work? How might a woman reader resist the male bias in a work?
- If the work leaves out women, how might one fill in the gaps? Can one add female characters and imagine their response to the action? (For example, where is Sarah when God tells Abraham to sacrifice his son?)
- Can female values be found in the male characters or embedded in the text? How can female readers resist male biases and make the works their own? How do the women characters react to their suppression by the patriarchy?
- Is the work "feminist" in that it seeks to show how the patriarchal system needs to be destroyed and replaced by a system that emphasizes more humane values?

- Does the work advocate certain "female" values, such as sharing, cooperativeness, caring for others, sensitivity to the needs of others, compassion?
- In examining works by female writers, what understanding and vision of life does one find? What do we learn about women from their own point of view? How does the work reflect women's culture, women's ways of thinking and feeling?
- How is the work part of women's traditions of literature? How does the work go beyond male conventions and genres of literature into new female directions?

Works Cited (with additional bibliography)

Beauvoir, Simone de. *The Second Sex*. Trans. and ed. H. M. Parshley. New York: Vintage, 1974.

Belsey, Catherine, and Jane Moore. eds. *The Feminist Reader: Essays in Gender and the Politics of Literary Criticism*. New York: Basil Blackwell, 1989.

Bronte, Charlotte. *Jane Eyre*. London: Oxford University Press, 1969.

Donovan, Josephine, ed. *Feminist Literary Criticism: Explorations in Theory*. 2nd ed. Lexington: University of Kentucky Press, 1989.

Donovan, Josephine. Ed. *Feminist Theory: The Intellectual Traditions of American Feminism*. New York: Frederick Ungar, 1985.

Doyle, James A. T*he Male Experience*. Dubuque: Wm. C. Brown, 1983.

Eisenstein, Hester. *Contemporary Feminist Thought*. Boston: G.K. Hall, 1983.

Fetterley, Judith. T*he Resisting Reader: A Feminist Approach to American Fiction*. Bloomington: Indiana University Press, 1977.

French, Marilyn. *Beyond Power: On Women, Men, and Morals*. New York: Ballantine Books, 1985.

Gilbert, Sandra and Susan Gubar. *The Madwoman in the Attic: The Woman Writer and the Nineteenth-century Imagination*. New Haven: Yale University Press, 1984.

Humm, Maggie. *Feminist Criticism: Women as Contemporary Critics*. Brighton: The Harvester Press, 1986.

Kolodny, Annette. "Dancing Through the Minefield." Showalter, *New Fem. Crit*. 144-159.

Millett, Kate. *Sexual Politics*. New York: Avon, 1971.

Pratt, Annis. *Archetypal Patterns In Women's Fiction*. Bloomington: Indiana University Press, 1981.

Rich, Adrienne. *Of Woman Born: Motherhood as Experience and Institution*. New York: Norton, 1976.

Register, Cheri. "American Feminist Literary Criticism: A Bibliographical Introduction." Donovan, *Fem Lit. Crit*, 1-28.

Ruthven, K.K. *Feminist Literary Studies: An Introduction*. Cambridge: Cambridge University Press, 1984.

Showalter, Elaine, ed. *The New Feminist Criticism: Essays on Women, Literature, and Theory*. New York: Pantheon Books, 1985.

---. "Feminist Criticism in the Wilderness." Showalter New Fem. Crit, 243-268.

---. "Toward a Feminist Poetics." *Women's Writing and Writing about Women*. Ed. Mary Jacobus. London: Croom Helm, 1979.

Spender, Dale. *The Writing or the Sex? or Why you Don't Have to Read Women's Writing to Know It's No Good*. New York: Pergamon Press, 1989.

Weedon, Chris. *Feminist Practice and Poststructuralist Theory*. Oxford: Basil Blackwell, 1987.

8

DECONSTRUCTION APPROACH
TO LITERATURE

INTRODUCTION TO DECONSTRUCTIONISM

Deconstruction derives from the work of Jacques Derrida, a French philosopher. But before we examine Derrida's ideas, it might be helpful to briefly consider some of the linguistic concepts of an earlier French writer, Ferdinand de Saussure.

According to Saussure, the linguistic unit, **the sign**, consists of two elements: the concept, referred to as **the signified**, and the sound-image, referred to as **the signifier**. For example, everyone has a concept of a large woody plant usually with a trunk and branches. In English the sound-image for this signified is the signifier *tree*. In Latin the sound-image for this signified is *arbor*: in German, the signifier is *baum*. "The bond," Saussure says, "between the signifier and the signified is arbitrary." There is no natural connection between the signifier and signified. The sign, "the whole that results from the associating of the signifier with the signified is arbitrary (67). How do we know the difference between a house [haus] and a horse [hors]? Obviously, when we are learning how to speak, one or more persons said horse when pointing to a four-legged large creature or maybe to its picture in a book. And people called a building in which people lived a house. If we called a horse a house, someone would have corrected us. But if we had been born in Italy, we would have called the animal *cavallo* [kavalo] and the building casa [kasa], and we would have learned how to distinguish between the two signs just as easily. The arbitrary connections between signifieds and signifiers, the signs, we learn from the community of speakers among whom we live.

A language is a system of signs shared by a community of speakers. Saussure emphasized **synchronic linguistics**, which is the study of language as it exists at a given time, contrasted to **diachronic linguistics**, which is the study of language as it changes and evolves. In synchronic linguistics, the system is complete at any given moment. Saussure defines language as a "system of interdependent terms in which the value of each term results solely from the simultaneous presence of the others … " (114). A sign has its meaning in relationship to all the other signs in the system.

Every sign is different from every other sign. A horse is not a house or a goose or a mouse or a force. A sign derives its meaning from what it is not as much as from what it is. A horse is a horse because it is not a house. Derrida says, "no element can function as a sign without referring to another element which itself is not simply present" (*Pos* 26). Each sign has in it traces of other signs—"everywhere, differences and traces of traces." The meaning of a sign depends on its difference from other signs, on the absence of other signs, on its relationship to other signs. The meaning of a sign depends on what context it is used in, and of course every context in which the sign is used is different. Thus, meaning is not stable but ever shifting, changing, "the spin-off of a potentially endless play of signifiers" (127), as Terry Eagleton puts it. Or as Derrida writes, "every concept is inscribed in a chain or in a system within which it refers to the other, to other concepts, by means of the systematic play of differences" ("Dif" 11).

Difference leads to *differance*, a word Derrida has invented, although he says it is neither a word nor a concept. *Differance* (in both French and English) sounds exactly like *difference*, but changing the *e* to an *a* relates differance to the French verb *differer*, which means both to differ and to defer, delay, or postpone. *Differance* is "the systematic play of differences"; it is the "playing movement that 'produces'—by means of something that is not simply an activity—these differences, these effects of differences" ("Dif" 11). Again, it is the difference between one sign and another that enables us to distinguish *horse* from *house*. *Differance* refers to the otherness of things, how things are related by being different as well as alike. Jane Tompkins explains *differance* as "that which allows us to think in terms of contrast/comparative relationships. It is the very possibility of thinking relationally, and, therefore, it couldn't itself ever appear. It is what enables other things to appear" (29).

Differance also suggests deferral, putting off, delaying, suspending. When no horse is present, but absent, we use the sign of horse in place of the horse itself: "The sign represents the present in its absence. It takes the place of the present. When we cannot grasp or show the thing, state the present, the being-present, when the present cannot be presented, we signify, we go through the detour of the sign … The sign, in this sense, is deferred presence" ("Dif" 9).

Another way of looking at "deferred presence" is to consider Jonathan Culler's example of the flight of the arrow based on the ancient paradox of

Zeno. At any instance in the flight of the arrow, the arrow is at a particular spot in space and thus never in motion. But the arrow does move: it hits an object or falls on the ground. If we look closer at that instant in which the arrow seems not to be moving, we can see that moment contains traces of the past flight of the arrow and traces of the future flight of the arrow. "The presence of motion is conceivable, it turns out, only insofar as every instant is already marked with the traces of the past and future" (94).

"Deferred presence" leads us, perhaps arbitrarily (but then any examination of the process of differance is arbitrary because there is no beginning or ending in differance or deconstruction) to the "metaphysics of presence," which Derrida says underlies all Western thinking. All Western metaphysics, going back at least to Aristotle, is based on the concept that there is a reality, there is truth, beyond, outside language. Language is a mechanism for expressing and representing truth. We believe there is a reality beyond words that we can express in words.

Another term that Derrida uses to describe Western thinking is **logocentrism**.

Logocentrism puts as the center the *logos*, which in Greek means "the word" or "reason." Culler defines it as "the orientation of philosophy toward an order of meaning—thought, truth, reason, logic, the Word—conceived of as existing in itself, as foundation" (92). Logocentrism puts meaning before language; meaning has an independent existence which language expresses. The words are a representation or expression of an idea or the Idea (Plato), a truth, the subjectivity of an individual, God, or what Derrida calls "the transcendental signified," "the presence of a value or a meaning supposedly antecedent to *differance*..." (*Pos* 29).

This concept, Sharon Crowley suggests, comes from our belief that we possess "an 'inner voice'—that voice (or consciousness, or memory) which assures each of us of our self-identity, indeed, of our 'self-present-ness'" (2). "I think; therefore I am" (Descartes). I am present to myself in the act of thinking. I remember the past, I anticipate the future, I am conscious of the present time. I feel a continuity of my past and present. I express myself to others and to me in language. I see me as a stable, unified self. Derrida's *differance* undoes this concept of the integrated, stable self or individual. Because the signs we use are the products of differance, of differing and deferring, because the signs derive their meaning by the absence of other signs, because the signs have meaning only in a system of other signs, and because as Eagleton puts it, "nothing is ever fully present in the signs," (129), the self cannot be fully present either. He explains it further:

[I]t is an illusion for me to believe that I can ever be fully present to you in what I say or write, because to use signs at all entails that my meaning is always somehow dispersed, divided, and never quite at one with itself. Not only my meaning, indeed, but me: since language is something I am made out of, rather than merely a convenient tool I use, the whole idea that I am a stable, unified entity must also be a fiction. Not only can I never be fully present to you, but I can never be fully present to myself either (130).

The individual, that is "the conscious and speaking subject," says Derrida, "depends upon the system of differences and the movement of *differance* [and] the subject is not present, nor above all present to itself before *differance* ... the subject is constituted only in being divided from itself, ... in deferral ... " (Pos 29).

Thus, the concept of the conscious, integrated individual as the center of Western thought is undermined. Logocentrism, which tries to deny *differance* by assuming the existence of something prior to differance, is also undermined. In Derridean thought there is nothing prior to *differance*. There is no "transcendental signified." There are no truths outside of the system of differences. "The absence of the transcendental signified," says Derrida, "extends the domain and the interplay of signification *ad infinitum*" ("Struct" 249).

From another angle what this means is that language is a system complete in itself. It doesn't refer to anything outside of itself. There are no transcendent truths outside of language. Jane Tompkins writes, "there is no transcendent truth present outside the field which governs the field in its totality because such a goal, some final master principle, would have to be thought within language and so would always be at stake, rather than governed" (31). Even consciousness, subjectivity, is formed by language. Language speaks us, so to speak.

Western thinking centered on reason, logocentrism, works by a hierarchy of **binary oppositions**. This is a "violent hierarchy," says Derrida, "One of the two terms governs the other (axiologically, logically, etc.), or has the upper hand" (Pos 41). Some examples are nature/culture; soul/body; man/woman; presence/ absence; conscious/unconscious—one could fill a book with binary oppositions important to Western thought. In each set of oppositions, as Gayatri Chakravorty Spivak points out in her introduction to Derrida's *Of Grammatology*, "The superior term belongs to presence and the logos; the inferior serves to define its status and mark a fall" (lxix). It is a hierarchy because one of the two terms is superior to the other, and a "violent" hierarchy because of the much greater priority given to the first term associated with reason, meaning, the logos. It is a "violent" hierarchy too because the first term suppresses, keeps under control the second term. It is the first term, the superior term, that serves as the center. The second term, the inferior term, opposes or negates the first term; it appears marginal, inessential. The superior term is "privileged." For example, in Western, logocentric thinking (feminists would say phallocentric), male is privileged over female. A 1991 movie which has a female director for the part of the movie focusing on the main female character and a male director for the part of the movie focusing on the main male character is listed thus in The New Yorker: "'He Said, She Said' (Ken Kwapis and Marisa Silver) [the directors], with Kevin Bacon, Elizabeth Perkins ..." Notice which sex appears first in each pair; guess the gender of the writer; guess which character is presented first, the man or the woman; guess which section lasts longer, the male's or the female's? (The answer is, of course, the same for all the questions.)

Deconstructing Text

Deconstruction is a process in which one seeks to undo, dismantle, overturn, deconstruct the hierarchy of the binary oppositions, let's say in a text. One reverses the two terms of the hierarchy so that the privileged term, the term belonging to presence, to the logos, to reason, is overturned in favor of the second term which appears to be marginal. Perhaps, rather than simply reversing the terms, one attempts to erase the borders, the dividing line between them. One decenters a text, removing the first term from the center and placing the marginal at the "center." To deconstruct," says Derrida, "is to overturn the hierarchy at a given moment" (*Pos* 41)—perhaps a moment in which the marginal intrudes, disrupts the surface, disturbs any supposed unity of the work.

Instead of deconstructing a text, what one may be doing is analyzing how a text is deconstructing itself. The binary oppositions in a text are not peacefully coexisting (Pos 41). The second, inferior term is always there in the background, the margin, threatening to dislocate the center, the dominance of the first term. What one looks out for are the moments in the text in which the text differs from itself, when it appears to contradict itself, or as Eagleton puts it, when texts "come to embarrass their own ruling logic" (133). "*Differance*," says Spivak, "invites us to undo the need for balanced equations, to see if each term in an opposition is not after all an accomplice of the other" (lix).

In one sense the concept of binary oppositions is an illusion, since the closer one examines the pair of binary oppositions in a work the more one can see that each term contains traces of the other and that the differences between the privileged terms and the inferior terms are not simple but complex. "The 'deconstruction' of a binary opposition," says Barbara Johnson, "is thus not an annihilation of all values or differences; it is an attempt to follow the subtle, powerful effects of differences already at work within the illusion of a binary opposition" (xi). It is the difference within a text that makes it impossible for a text to have a "unique identity"; it is the difference within a text that infinitely defers "the possibility of adding up the sum of a text's parts or meanings and reaching a totalized, integrated whole" (4). The work is self-contradictory; the meaning of the work is divided against itself. A text has no single meaning but multiple meanings. "The de-construction" of a text proceeds by "the careful teasing out of warring forces of signification with the text itself" (5).

So, how do we go about deconstructing a literary text? Even in a first reading we are aware of some contradictions in a text, of some elements in the text that seem to jar us, that don't seem to fit in. Close rereadings will show us other points of disturbance. We need to ask questions like these: What are the binary oppositions at work in the text? Which of the two terms is favored? What are the moments in the text in which the inferior term refuses to be suppressed but makes itself felt? "Undecidables" is a word that Derrida uses to describe such moments that disrupt the hierarchy of binary oppositions. Spivak suggests that in reading we look out for a word "that seems to harbor an unresolvable contradiction," one that seems to mean one thing in one part of the text and something else in another part. We should watch out for a metaphor "that seems to suppress its implications." She emphasizes that we are not looking for examples of ambiguity or irony but "a moment that genuinely threatens to collapse that system" (lxxv). What are the holes, the gaps, the absences, in the text that we feel a need to fill in? Does the juxtaposition of certain elements in the structure of the text disjoint the text in some way? We are examining how the text differs from itself. We bring what appears to be marginal to the center—decentering is another way of referring to the process of deconstruction. A practical way to get started might be to examine a critical essay that discusses the theme of a work or which indicates the unity of a work, and then determine what the essay leaves out, what it ignores.

According to Spivak deconstruction follows this formula: "To locate the promising marginal text, to disclose the undecidable moment, to pry it loose with the positive lever of the signifier; to reverse the resident hierarchy, only to displace it; to dismantle in order to reconstitute what is always already inscribed. Deconstruction in a nutshell" (lxxvii). Having dislodged the privileged term and thus reversed the hierarchy of binary oppositions, we have not completed the process of deconstruction. The previously privileged term is "reinscribed," not destroyed. What has been reversed can be reversed again—and again. The phase of overturning, says Derrida, "is the necessity of an interminable analysis: the hierarchy of dual oppositions always reestablishes itself" (Pos 42). Finally, there is no "finally" in deconstruction.

An Experiment In Literary Deconstruction

"The Lamb" from *Songs of Innocence* by William Blake

Little Lamb who made thee
Dost thou know who made thee
Gave thee life & bid thee feed,
By the stream & o'er the mead:
Gave thee clothing of delight,
Softest clothing wooly bright;
Gave thee such a tender voice,
Making all the vales rejoice:
Little Lamb who made thee
Dost thou know who made thee

Little Lamb I'll tell thee.
Little Lamb I'll tell thee:
He is called by thy name,
For he calls himself a Lamb:
He is meek & he is mild,
He became a little child:
I a child & thou a Lamb,
We are called by his name.
Little Lamb God bless thee
Little Lamb God bless thee

In the first stanza of William Blake's "The Lamb," the speaker, a child, asks the lamb simple questions, but without question marks. Does the little lamb know who made him? The speaker seems to think the lamb is innocent and ignorant. The speaker suggests that the maker of the lamb has given the lamb life, provides for all of his needs, including food and clothing. The maker of the lamb has given him a "tender voice,/ Making all the vales rejoice," suggesting that the lamb's voice is part of the joy of nature. Everything in this stanza seems to suggest harmony, innocence, peace. The last two lines repeat the first two lines, but now the questions "Little Lamb who made thee / Dost thou know who made thee" are already partly answered. The maker of the lamb is kind, loving, generous, and protective.

In the second stanza, the speaker tells the lamb that its maker calls himself a Lamb. The maker of the lamb, the Lamb, is like the lamb, "meek and mild." The Lamb became a little child. The speaker, the child, sees a unity among the child ("I a child") and the lamb ("thou a lamb) and the Lamb who became a child ("We are called by his name"). He ends by saying, "Little Lamb God bless thee" twice. The last two lines seem to answer the first two lines of the poem. God is mentioned and the speaker wishes God to bless the lamb suggesting both present and future care of the lamb by God. All is harmony and peace.

In traditional Christian symbolism the Lamb of God is Jesus, the Son of God, the Savior. In the Gospel of John he is identified as "The Lamb of God who takes away the sin of the world." In the poem the speaker tells us that the Lamb "became a little child," referring to the incarnation. Jesus is "meek and mild" and tenderly loves the lamb and the child (the speaker).

Now, are there any jarring notes in this sweet and simple poem where even the rhythm is smooth and reassuring? Is there some moment which overturns the speaker's vision of peace and harmony? Is the speaker really as undivided and whole as he appears? Are there gaps, holes in the text that we fill in with opposing viewpoints? What questions do we ask that the speaker doesn't ask? How does the text differ from itself?

I'll begin with a couple of lines that I have always found disturbing: "Gave thee clothing of delight/ Softest clothing wooly bright." The "clothing" is the lamb's wool—but I ask to whom is the lamb's clothing a "delight"? The lamb is still wearing the wool, but "softest clothing wooly bright" sounds more like a sweater which the speaker, the child, might wear once the lamb is shorn as it surely will be. "Clothing" is worn only by human beings (soft clothing would feel good against our bare skin). There would be no "clothing" for a naked lamb, shorn of its coat. "Wooly" would keep us warm in the winter; "bright" would make the garment made of wool attractive. Will the lamb stripped of his fur be as "blessed" as he is now? Will the lamb also be castrated, as lambs often are? Then will his tender voice make all the vales rejoice? Even if the lamb is not castrated, will his "tender voice" always be one of joy? Surely lambs, like all creatures, cry out more from suffering than from pleasure.

Let's go back earlier in the poem. If the maker of the lamb gives life to the lamb, doesn't he also take it away? Will the lamb always be fed and watered in abundance? The setting of the poem seems to be spring, but will not winter follow when the meadow will not be filled with grass? Hunger and thirst are absent in the poem, but perhaps are suggested by their very absence. And the lamb will inevitably experience hunger and thirst, perhaps castration, ultimately death. Will he slaughtered and eaten, turned to mutton for the child to eat? What happened to the "meek and mild" Lamb of God?

And is the speaker really as innocent as he appears? Doesn't he have, at least on the unconscious level, some understanding of the fate of the lamb—his wool turned into clothing, his body turned into food for people? Farm kids know what happens to farm animals. And underneath all the harmony and peace of the poem perhaps there are traces of the insecurity of life and the fear of death.

And what about the other lamb in the poem, the maker of the lamb, who "calls himself a Lamb"? If he became a little child, did he not grow up to die on the cross? The "meek and mild" Lamb is the sacrificial lamb, "the Lamb that was slain" (Rev. 5:12); "he is brought as a lamb to the slaughter" (Is. 53:7). If the maker and protector of the lamb was himself slain, sacrificed, how can the lamb be safe and secure?

Let's return to the main question of the poem: Who made the lamb? In reading just the first stanza, the answer is obvious—God. But the second stanza tells us the Lamb, who "became a little child," made the lamb, that is, Jesus, the Son of God, Christ ("we are called by his name"—Christians?). "God" appears only in the last two lines in the form of a blessing the little boy gives to the lamb. Is there some division in the unity of God? (Perhaps the paradox of the Trinity inserts itself here, or is this Blake's own peculiar theology?)

"Did he who made the Lamb make thee?" Blake asks in the companion poem to "The Lamb" in his Songs of Experience. Did the Lamb make the tiger? To turn the question around somewhat, are there qualities of the tiger in the lamb, or in the Lamb?

What I may have been doing in the above paragraphs is reversing the hierarchy of the pair of binary oppositions: innocence/experience. In the poem innocence is the privileged term; experience is the inferior term. But there are traces of experience in innocence, just as there would be traces of innocence in experience. One of the many things I've omitted in this analysis is the concept of salvation suggested by the last five lines. Because the Lamb became a little child, "we are called by his name" and are blessed. The Lamb's sacrificial death brings salvation. But there would be no need for salvation if there were not a fall from innocence. Perhaps the poem is about the longing for an innocence that exists only in language, for the transcendental signified.

I am going to stop here and not because I am finished. There is no end to the making of further questions and to answers which would lead to more questions. One could, for example, reverse the hierarchy of male/ female in the poem. Notice that I have referred to the child as male while the poem does not (the water color picture Blake combines with the text shows us a naked boy); but what would happen if one thought of the child, the lamb, and even God as female? And also I have referred to the lamb as male, although the text gives no indication of the sex of the lamb. One could go on and on. But I have other things to do. So do you.

Works Cited

Some of these books, particularly Culler's, contain helpful bibliographies. All of these books [except for Derrida's] are accessible to the beginning reader of deconstruction.

Crowley, Sharon. *A Teacher's Introduction to Deconstruction.* Urbana: National Council of Teachers of English, 1989.
Culler, Jonathan. *On Deconstruction: Theory and Criticism after Structuralism.* Ithaca: Cornell University Press, 1982.
Derrida, Jacques. "Differance." *Margins of Philosophy.* Trans. Alan Bass. Chicago: University of Chicago Press, 1982.
--- . *Positions.* Trans. Alan Bass. Chicago: University of Chicago Press, 1981.
---. "Structure, Sign, and Play in the Discourse of the Human Sciences." *The Structuralist Controversy.* Ed. Richard Macksey and Eugenio Donato. Baltimore: Johns Hopkins University Press, 1970.
Eagleton, Terry. *Literary Theory: An Introduction.* Minneapolis: University of Minnesota Press, 1983.
Johnson, Barbara. *The Critical Difference.* Baltimore: The Johns Hopkins University Press, 1980.
Saussure, Ferdinand de. *Course in General Linguistics.* Ed. Charles Bally, Albert Sechehaye, and Albert Riedlinger. Trans. Wade Baskin. New York : McGraw-Hill Book Co., 1986.
Spivak, Gayatri Chakravorty. Translator's Preface. By Jacques Derrida. *Of Grammatology.* Baltimore: Johns Hopkins Press, 1976.
Tompkins. Jane. "A Short Course in Post-Structuralism." *Conversations.* Ed. Charles Moran and Elizabeth F. Penfield. Urbana: National Council of Teachers of English,1990.

9

"ANOTHER CULTURE" APPROACH
TO LITERATURE

I used to teach a literature course in which students read literature from a non-Western culture. The purpose of the course was to introduce students to another culture partly to increase their understanding and appreciation of another culture and partly to examine their own culture in contrast to a culture that may be very different from their own. I usually began with a book that was as close to their own culture as I could find. Since most of my students were from small-town rural America, they could identify easily with Garrison Keillor's Lake Wobegone stories or Roger Welsch's stories about a small town in Nebraska. A few students from big cities found life in Lake Wobegone or Centralia somewhat alien, but most students found these towns just like their own home towns, where everybody knows what everybody else is up to. After reading and talking about how these stories reveal the everyday life and culture of small town America, we journeyed to ancient India and read R.K. Narayan's version of *The Ramayana*, an ancient epic which is still a vital part of modern Indian culture. Most of the rest of the course was devoted to modern novels and short stories and films which gave us some understanding of both how life in India is different from life in America and yet how people there share many of the same problems and same hopes, dreams, problems and fears that we do. I liked to conclude with a novel which brought the two cultures together—like Bharati Mukerjee's *Jasmine*, in which a woman from India adjusts to living in New York and Iowa. I primarily used the following approaches in the course: (a) using contemporary American literature, we examined our own culture by trying to look at it objectively, almost as if it were another culture; (b) primarily using literature from another culture, we looked both for basic differences and similarities in order to gain some understanding and appreciation of the other culture; and (c) we applied other approaches, such as Freudian, archetypal, and feminist, to another culture's literature to deepen our understanding of that literature. The remainder of this chapter will examine these approaches at length and discuss how they might be applied in a classroom setting.

EXAMINING ONE'S OWN CULTURE THROUGH LITERATURE

Start with a book as close to our own culture as possible. Choosing such a book is not easy because even if one found a novel about life in the very town where most students lived, there would be some students from somewhere else who would not find the culture described in the book very familiar. And the problem of choosing a book would be even harder, let's say, if the school is located in a city where students come from many different backgrounds. However, we have to start somewhere; and the more diverse the students the easier it might be to see the cultural differences expressed in the book. One method is to divide students into small groups and ask them to look at a short story or two or part of a novel and discuss first the similarities they found in the work to their own culture. How is life in the story like life in their home town or neighborhood? Do the characters resemble people they know? Students usually like to tell stories of their own which parallel the stories in the book. My students usually enjoyed telling stories about how everybody in their small town knows everybody's business. (Even my student from Calcutta told how everybody in his neighborhood knew when he came home very late.) Then one can ask them to discuss what they find different or strange in the work. Students from big cities sometimes find life in a small town very remote from their own experience. Another method is to pretend to be from another culture and try to see what is alien in the culture described in the book. One might even pretend to be Mr. Spock and analyze the aspects in the culture which seem illogical.

Frequently, in a work of fiction there is one character who is in conflict with her or his culture, a character who doesn't fit in, who feels estranged from the others in her or his community. If we probe these characters' discomfort and alienation, we can reach a deeper understanding of how the culture works.

Every culture, every community puts pressure on people to conform to its expectations, its unwritten laws. The most common oral expression of this pressure is, "What will the neighbors think? What will people say?" People growing up in a community automatically absorb the precepts, the conventions of their community. Individuals are trained to accept and to comply with the norms of their community. It is helpful in studying any culture to see how the culture makes people feel good if they follow its rules and guilty if they don't. Thus, one needs to examine in a work of literature what pressures the culture is putting on the characters. What are the characters expected to practice and to avoid? How does a community make persons feel shame and disgrace if they go against its regulations? And how does the community reward those who adhere to its demands? Analyzing how individuals are trying to adjust to the expectations of their community will help us to comprehend and appreciate the difficulties and the choices the characters make.

Culture is a broad term that includes what a people believe, what their shared values are, what their everyday life is like, what they do for fun and amusement, what kind of family life and family structure is dominant, what gender roles people are expected to follow, etc. Trying to describe how we live in our own culture is good preparation for moving to another culture.

At the end of this unit I asked students to write a letter to someone, perhaps from another culture, who is moving to this fictional town. The writer could pretend to be either a longtime resident or someone who has moved there in the last few months. The following questions could be adapted to almost any fiction: What is everyday life like for the people of this community? What kind of problems would a newcomer have in adjusting to life here? What kind of sense of community exists? What kind of work ethic do the people follow? What do the people do for fun and pleasure? What kind of problems do they have? What is family life like? What is the role of women? What does it mean to be a "man" in this community? What tensions and conflicts exist in the community? What can you say about the religion of the people here? What rituals and holidays do the people practice and celebrate? What do people consider to be the most important things in their life? (This is, of course, not a comprehensive set of questions. There are many other questions one could ask. And no one could be expected to write on all of these without composing a book.)

Finally, in writing about any culture one needs to qualify one's generalizations. Cultures, like individuals, are complex, and one should avoid saying everything is true about everybody. For example, don't write, "Everyone in my town loves football." Write: "most people" or "some people." Sweeping generalizations are not only false but dangerous.

EXPERIENCING ANOTHER CULTURE THROUGH LITERATURE

Why study another culture anyway? Here I am in the middle of a continent in what many Americans claim is the richest and most powerful country in the world where everyone speaks English, and there are no foreigners in my home town.

But there are. Yesterday, I saw a little boy from India playing with his scooter on the sidewalk across the street. Last week in the local supermarket, I heard people speaking Spanish and Chinese. If I turn on the television I can hear of cultural conflicts all over the world. We live in a multi-cultural society, which is becoming more and more culturally diverse; we live on a planet where peoples of many different cultures find themselves in closer and closer contact. We need to understand and even appreciate other cultures. If we get to know people of other cultures and understand some of their customs and their ways of approaching life, our fear of the "other" may disappear. And we might find that a study of other cultures will enrich us.

Another reason for the study of another culture is that such an exploration may result in self-discovery and self-development. I think we cannot understand what it means to be American unless we have been Americans in Paris or Americans in Bangkok. It is impossible to investigate another culture without comparing it to our own. We become more aware of our own identities as Americans as we learn what it means to be Chinese or Indian. And if we try to understand the pressures and expectations another culture puts on its people, we might better understand how we too are affected by our culture.

Another reason I like to study other cultures is that I find such reading fascinating. I used to read a lot of science fiction because I enjoy reading about imaginary exotic cultures located on distant planets or in the future. I have discovered that our own planet is wonderfully diverse.

The best way to experience another culture would be to live in another country, learn the language, and share the life of the people in a community. But if we cannot pack our bags and go to India for a year, we can go on a journey through literature, a journey that can take us not only to present-day India but to the past. Literature can take us to places where a traveler or a even a longtime resident could not enter—we can go inside people's homes, even inside their minds to see how they think and feel. We can experience their culture to some extent as they themselves experience it.

The methods and questions we used in examining our own culture can be used to study another culture. We can examine a novel, a short story, a poem, a play and discuss what in the work seems familiar to us, what appears to us be universally human. Almost always, we will find human beings like ourselves, sharing our basic needs for food, shelter, love. We will often find characters who will remind us of people we know. We may discover that life in a small village in India will in some ways resemble life in a small town in Nebraska. Then we can discuss what seems to be alien, strange, different from our culture. We may frequently conclude that what seems odd at first appears more comprehensible, even more human, as we see the odd action in the larger context of the culture. In looking at the differences, we need to keep an open mind and avoid jumping to premature conclusions; we need to develop tolerance of other people's ways of doing things and approaching life. We need an active curiosity as we look at the diverse ways human beings think, behave and live together. Above all, we need to restrain ourselves from always concluding that these differences indicate the superiority of our own culture. Maybe it will be better if when we are discussing differences, we try to avoid making value judgments and concentrate at the beginning, at least, on understanding and appreciating the differences. And we need to be careful about making sweeping generalizations based on insufficient evidence. Instead of making generalizations about India based on one short story, let us make generalizations just about the character or the particular community in which the story takes place.

Other methods we used in looking at our own culture can be applied to other cultures. Main characters in a work of fiction usually have problems in dealing with their culture. Examining how these characters deal with their conflicts with their culture will reveal much about the culture itself. We can probe how individuals struggle with the pressures their culture puts on them to conform to its code of behavior. For example, we may see how an educated woman finds herself repressed by the traditional limited role of women in her culture. We can see how characters' behavior can be explained by their culture's concepts of shame and honor. The more we read the more we will understand the everyday life of the people, their work, their play, their family structure and family relationships, their religion, their shared values, *etc*. And in most cases we will see that their culture is not static but constantly changing. Most cultures, including our own, are in a transition between the traditional and the modern. Non-western cultures struggle between holding on to their own traditional ways and assimilating the ways of the West.

Another approach is to take certain concepts of a culture and see how they can be found in different works. For example, I used the term "dharma" as an organizing principle for my course in Indic literature. Dharma is a complex, profound concept that cannot easily be translated. It suggests moral law, righteousness, the path of right conduct, duty. One's dharma depends on one's class or caste, one's age, one's stage in life, one's sex, one's responsibilities to other members of one's family. Thus, everyone has a somewhat different dharma to follow. And in each work one can consider how the characters live up to their dharma. One could also apply the term to someone in our own culture.

Literature itself is only part of a culture. We will frequently need historical background and some understanding of geography. Learning to appreciate the art and music of a culture will deepen and enrich our understanding of the culture.

APPLYING OTHER APPROACHES TO THE LITERATURE OF ANOTHER CULTURE

So far we have been focusing on understanding another culture by examining how the literature reveals the culture as being similar or contrasting to our own. But any approach that we use to analyze literature (like those described in this book, for example) may also be helpful both in looking at a particular piece of literature and in learning about the culture in which the literature takes place.

Traditional approaches emphasizing the lives and times of authors and their place in literary history give us insight into the writers' culture. Any summaries of authors' lives will tell us something about how they fit into their own culture. Finding out about writers' early family life, the expectations of their parents, the kind of education writers received—all of these things will help us to see writers as part of a culture. Biographies, like fiction, deal with the everyday life of people, emphasizing the problems and pleasures of individuals as they adjust to their culture.

Literary history puts a work into the context of the literary tradition of its culture. How is the work a part of a literary movement of a country or a region? How is the writer reacting against current literary practices of the time? How does the work follow the traditional genres or types of literature of the culture? What literary conventions is a writer expected to follow? How have writers adapted literary forms from another culture to their own? For example, in writing a novel, a Western type of fiction is used by writers all over the world. How much or how little has an author incorporated fictional techniques unique to her or his own culture? Many novelists, such as native American writers, include oral traditions and methods of storytelling and mythological frameworks in their fiction.

Moreover, we may need to adjust genre descriptions of poetry, fiction, and drama to the literature of other cultures. Every culture has its own poetic figures of speech, conventional symbols, and metrical devices—not all of which can be translated into another language. Western concepts of tragedy and comedy may not work with plays of India and China. But many of our methods in analyzing our own literature will aid us in our reading of other literature. Discussing how the setting adds to the story, how the characters conflict with their societies, and how point of view works in the fiction will broaden our understanding of the story and of the culture in which the story takes place.

Freud's concept of the above-I (super-ego) can be useful when we consider how individuals internalize the pressures their culture puts upon them. Remember that Freud says the above-I "becomes the vehicle of tradition and of the all the time-restraining judgements of value which have propagated themselves in this manner from generation to generation." We can better comprehend the behavior of individuals when we consider they must deal not only with their external world—parents urging them to get married and settle down, friends making fun of them when they do something unusual, insisting that they live up to society's demands and punishing them when they do not. Closely related to Freud's concept of the above-I is Jung's persona—the conformity archetype, the public roles individuals are expected to play in their culture.

Looking for archetypal images, persons, and patterns in literature of another culture can help us to appreciate what in that culture is universally human. If we probe how the archetypes work in the context of another culture, we may also perceive the differences in that culture. Heroes' archetypal journeys are partly an initiation into their cultures. Initiation into womanhood or manhood in particular will vary with cultures. And we may discover that what we thought was a universal symbol is really a cultural symbol.

The feminist approach can be used to study how the patriarchal system works in another culture, perhaps even more obviously than in our own. We can think about how the culture determines gender roles, what it expects of males and females. We can examine how the culture inhibits women and how it may in some ways enable them to reach self-fulfillment. We can explore the roles women are expected to play, as daughters, wives, mothers, and workers. If we conclude that the culture discriminates against women, we might look again at how our culture treats women. We also can explore the roles expected of men in the culture. We may see, for example, that an honor code forces men to conform to a rigid code of manliness that represses some of their basic human qualities. We can also look for feminist values in the literature and in the culture. The other culture may be more spiritual and less materialistic than our own.

As one can see, these approaches overlap and complement one another. Applying them to literature of another culture may help us to understand another culture and perhaps even deepen our appreciation of literature.

INDEX